SANJAY C. PATEL

GOD is REAL

The Stunning New Convergence
of Science and Spirituality

PURPLEWATER PAPERBACKS

PURPLEWATER PAPERBACKS LLC
4771 Sweetwater Blvd., Suite 333
Sugar Land, TX 77479, USA

Website: www.SanjayCPatel.com

Cover front and rear by Sanjay C. Patel. A Sage or Yogi Connects to God and the Universe.
Wave by Agsandrew, istockphoto.com; Yoga outline, by Â© (2011) Jupiterimages Corporation,
clipart.com.

Patel, Sanjay C.
God is real : the stunning new convergence of science and spirituality /
Sanjay C. Patel
Includes bibliographical references and index.
1. Religion and science. 2. God. 3. Apologetics. 4. Cosmology – Yoga – Bible – Genesis. I. Title.

ISBN-13: 978-0-9822267-1-1
ISBN-10: 0-9822267-1-3

Note & Disclaimer: All contents of this book constitute the author's opinions only. Without limiting the generality of the foregoing, all contents of this publication are provided for informational purposes only and are not a substitute for professional advice. The contents of this book have not been evaluated by the Food and Drug Administration or any other legally recognized professional organization. No information given in this publication is intended to diagnose, treat, cure, mitigate or prevent any disease, condition, or circumstance. Always consult your medical doctor before practicing any kind of alternative or adjunct therapy, supplement, or medicine. Neither the publisher nor the author assumes any responsibility for errors, or for changes that occur after publication, or for any information published by third-party sources and websites referenced in this publication.

To His Holiness Pramukh Swami Maharaj
who taught me the true art of Yoga
and whose insight and blessings
led to these paradigm-breaking discoveries.

ACKNOWLEDGEMENTS

I would like to take this opportunity to thank the following individuals for their valuable contribution.

Firstly, I am grateful to Dr. J. J. Raval, astrophysicist and President of the Indian Planetary Society, India, who encouraged me to get my research on ancient Yoga texts describing "*Deep-Sea Volcanoes and Their Associated Hydrothermal Vents*" published in a peer-reviewed science journal. Also helpful were my many discussions with Professor Pankaj S. Joshi, astrophysicist, Tata Institute of Fundamental Research (TIFR), India. Both of these scientists had reviewed an earlier manuscript of this book.

I am also thankful for the suggestions of various scientists who fact-checked the scientific narrative of the current book. Section 1 on *Volcanoes Under the Sea* was reviewed by an Earth scientist who preferred to remain anonymous. Section 2 on *A Brief History of Life on Earth* was reviewed by Dr. Lowell Dingus, Division of Paleontology, the American Museum of Natural History. Sections 3 and 4 on *The Big Bang, Our Galaxy, and Universe* were reviewed by Curator and Professor Mordecai-Mark Mac Low, Department of Astrophysics, the American Museum of Natural History. It should be made clear, however, that these scientists did not review the convergences I have drawn between Science and Spirituality. They reviewed the scientific material alone.

I also thank my wife, Prity, for her frank comments and unswerving support. Finally and most importantly, I thank my spiritual mentor His Holiness Pramukh Swami Maharaj for inspiring me to embark on this profound voyage of discovery.

"Things that are inaccessible
to the likes of you in experience ...
though they exist,
seem inconsistent when spoken of
by the likes of me."

– ancient Yogi, Vasishta

Yoga Vasishta 6.2.59.38

"Now the natural man doesn't receive
the things of God's Spirit,
for they are foolishness to him,
and he can't know them,
because they are spiritually discerned."

– Apostle Paul

Bible, 1 Corinthians 2:14

CONTENTS

INTRODUCTION

WE ARE AT THE DAWN OF SOMETHING UNPRECEDENTED: The stunning new convergence of modern science and ancient spirituality. There is a clear confluence that shows *God exists.*

It all culminates from a trail of 'coincidences' that began in 1985, in India. In my soul, I had received a spiritual calling and arrived there from London, UK, aspiring for enlightenment.

During this period, I lived and studied as a monk at a traditional ashram and seminary. Surrounded by hundreds of miles of barren land, the ashram was an oasis ornate with dancing peacocks and playful parakeets. A small village in itself, it was totally isolated from the world. It had its own well on which we were dependent for water. It also had its own fields where corn, wheat, barley, sugarcane, and various vegetables were grown. At the back of the ashram orange butterflies courted a garden of red roses. At its center was a thatched hut for meditation.

The whole ashram was self-sufficient. Everything from cooking, cleaning, to harvesting was performed by monks. However, our electricity supply was sporadic and we often sweltered in the summer heat. The ashram had no air-conditioning and only a few fans.

They were useless, of-course, when there was no power. Nevertheless, life was great.

Under the guidance of my spiritual mentor His Holiness Pramukh Swami Maharaj, I began a five-year academic and practical education in Theology, Sanskrit, and Yoga. During this time, I found myself perplexed with questions about the spiritual path and various concepts of God. Why is there so much suffering in the world? Why are there natural disasters? Why do bad things happen – especially to good people and the faithful? How will the poor eat? When will war and terrorism end? If God is all-powerful why doesn't he bring wrongdoers to justice? If God loves us why doesn't he fix everything with a snap of his finger?

His Holiness sat with me for hours upon end, numerous times, lovingly, intellectually, and reassuringly giving me answers. Sometimes, when I approached him with much reverence, he told me to regard him not as a guru but a friend; that ultimately I had to become my own guru and resolve for myself the many minutiae about which I questioned him; that many questions would resolve themselves as I meditated and practiced yoga; that the vexations of the mind would cease slowly with their practice; that the questions would be resolved not through wordy explanations but a transcendental spiritual experience.

His eyes were always filled with great compassion.

After one such session, as I was about to leave his room, he asked: "What books do you read?" I explained I couldn't read much apart from the university textbooks and other material that were part of my studies at the seminary. The professors and acharyas (traditional scholars) who were teaching our courses made it difficult to find time even for worship and service! "You have to make sure you don't miss out on any of these," he said firmly. "And study science in depth too, so that you can understand and explain ancient literature from a scientific perspective. Practice yoga regularly."

I had sensed in his eyes that he knew much more than he was

revealing. But how could there be a convergence between science and spirituality? Were they not mutually exclusive? *There can't be anything in the ancient Yoga Literature that would make scientific sense. Most of it is so exotic it has got to be transcendental and referring to some other dimension,* I thought. The seven day description of creation in the Bible didn't make much sense, either. It too, I concluded, would remain beyond the scope of human understanding forever.

I began to learn the art of yoga, but it was a while before I could begin my study of science. This was mainly due to the paucity of scientific literature in the ashram's library and I hadn't a clue even where to begin.

Two years later, this suddenly changed.

I read a fascinating article about underwater volcanoes and associated hot water springs called 'hydrothermal vents' deep within the world's oceans. The piece had appeared in a U.S.-based magazine that had somehow found its way to the ashram.

Here, right before my eyes, was the first definitive evidence of a convergence between science and spirituality!

"How?" You may ask. Well, like science, ancient Yoga Literature also describes great fires with associated water springs deep within the world's oceans. They are called *Vadavanala Agni.* The surprising thing is that these descriptions are thousands of years old whereas science made the discovery relatively recently.

But here's the really surprising part. The ancient 'Yogis' (or people who had mastered yoga) said the submarine fire drinks the sea's salty water. It then *removes salt* from the water before expelling it back into the ocean. Does science agree?

I took the article to another monk, a physicist and friend. He was intrigued by it and we decided to write to its author. "We think our ancient spiritual literature bears parallels to the modern discovery of submarine volcanoes and hydrothermal vents. Is water emerging from these vents depleted of its salt content?" We received a rather curt reply to this effect: "There is no correspondence between your spiritual literature and modern science."

That ended the matter for my friend, but I was suspicious of the scientist's response. Could we trust this man? Was he really being objective like a good scientist should be? Or was he burying his head in the sand like the proverbial ostrich because he felt insecure by what we showed him? Was he biased against spirituality? Was he prejudiced against India? Was he being completely truthful to us?

Several years passed and, in 1991, I graduated from my studies and yoga training. Now I had time to visit science institutes and consult directly with experts. Thumbing through numerous science journals and textbooks, I compared them with my studies of the *Vadavanala Agni,* the salt-removing submarine fire described by the ancient Yogis. Little did I realize this research would take me from the bottom of Earth's oceans to the ends of the cosmos, and from the beginnings of time to the dissolution of our universe trillions of eons in the future!

Now, I bring these major new convergences before you. In my thirty years of study, I've dedicated the last ten years specifically to the oceanography and cosmology of the Bible and ancient Yoga Literature. It turns out that the Yogis' descriptions of the submarine fire converge with science on not just one, but *twenty* counts! And yes, contrary to what we were told by the above scientist, water expelled from hydrothermal vents *is* depleted of its salt.[1] There *is* a correspondence between ancient spiritual literature and modern science!

Fortunately, not all scientists have an anti-spiritual worldview. There were many outstanding scientists who were happy to work with me on my new research. Working under the guidance of several oceanographers, geologists, and two astrophysicists,[2] I submitted the research for publication in reputed science journals.

"Publish or perish," one of them explained. "Peer-review is the hallmark of science. If the convergences are credible and important, they should get published, even if they come from ancient spiritual literature." The paper was accepted!

It appeared in three international journals and was presented at the 22nd International Congress on the History of Science.[3]

The convergences of science and ancient spirituality are rock solid. They are genuine. But don't take my word for it. See for yourself. *You* be the judge.

I began as an incorrigible skeptic, a grand doubter, who like the fabled doll of salt that ventured to test the depths of the ocean, was dissolved into it. Similar to the doll, to fathom the imagery, symbols, and metaphors of the Bible and the ancient Yoga Literature, you need to become as subtle as their passages and as fluid as their poetry.

This book will do that for you, bequeathing you a sumptuous inside view of the ancient passages. All you need do is sit back and read. I do not even ask you to open your mind. If it's not already, the convergences in this book will do that for you. The parallels of the Bible, the Yoga Literature, and modern science are extensive. Every follower of religion, every skeptic of spirituality, and every proponent of science should contemplate and witness for themselves these tremendous convergences and their implications.

The scope of these convergences also includes the worldwide flood and extinction of life described in the Bible as well as its 'seven day' synopsis of creation. Largely unobserved, both narratives have striking counterparts in ancient Yoga Literature. The Yoga Literature contains similar descriptions, only in much more detail. These additional particulars correspond with science on twenty counts. One of these includes the catastrophe's exact timeframe: Between 429-120 million years ago. Science confirms that there was indeed massive flooding and an extinction episode – the worst in Earth's history – during that very same period.

The precision of dates in the Yoga Literature is amazing. These impressive descriptions leave no doubt as to what the Bible describes. In view of this, the descriptions of a great flood in Genesis must refer to the same cataclysmic episode described by the Yoga Literature – and science.

Now, concerning creation. After my work appeared in the three journals and was warmly welcomed at the International Congress, I decided to pursue the correspondences beyond our planet into the universe. I found that the ancient Yogis described the creation of a spherical cosmic world called a *brahmanda*. Its description is similar to that of the world given in Genesis. Only, it's much more detailed. I found these details correspond to our ancient and enormous Milky Way Galaxy and the birth of our universe on 60 counts!

How can this be by chance? Again, one of these details includes *when* this huge cosmic world formed. Answer: Sometime between 14.9-10.6 billion years ago. Science corroborates our Galaxy indeed formed within the same time period.

When we view the Bible from this new perspective, too, Genesis suddenly exhibits 21 major convergences with our Galaxy. If you're not sure what our Galaxy is, don't worry. It's quite simple and I will show it to you with pictures and illustrations in Section 3. Then, in Section 5, you will see that the sequence of creation Genesis describes links together like a necklace of sparkling pearls! Moreover, a new understanding of each day of its seven-day timeline reveals a chronology that syncs perfectly with modern figures. Amongst the many new correct timelines that emerge, it also derives the exact age of our Sun: 4.6 billion years old.

All this isn't by chance. Too many convergences have emerged to allow that. There aren't just two or three, but over *one hundred.* So many new similarities have emerged that the convergence of science and spirituality is staggering. These colossal convergences cannot arise by accident. They're a major breakthrough in the 'science versus spirituality' debate and are a complete game-changer.

IMPOSSIBLE BECOMES POSSIBLE

THE GARGANTUAN WORLDVIEW of the ancient Yogis hasn't gone unnoticed by scientists. Some, such as Nobel physicists Erwin Schrodinger and Werner Heisenberg, and the distinguished astrophysicists Carl Sagan and Fritjof Capra, have brought it to light briefly in their papers and publications since 1945. Says Capra: "This idea of a periodically expanding and contracting universe, which involves a scale of time and space of vast proportions, has arisen not only in modern cosmology, but also in ancient Indian mythology ... evolutionary cosmologies which come very close to our modern scientific models."[4] Said Sagan: "It is the only religion in which the time scales correspond, no doubt by accident, to those of modern scientific cosmology. Its cycles run ... longer than the age of the Earth or the Sun and about half the time since the Big Bang. And there are much longer time scales still."[5]

Though Sagan was correct about the ancient Yoga Literature, it seems his view of the other great traditions is mistaken. The ancient Yogis weren't the only ones to get the big picture right. So did the ancient Israelites. More on this later.

The range of topics the ancient Yogis discussed is vast – from the world of atoms to the oceans, and from the Sun and stars to the Milky Way Galaxy, and from the Big Bang to infinite space.

All of these topics will be laid out before you in simple terms with ample illustrations. No previous knowledge of science will be required to understand them. Moreover, there is little mathematics in these discoveries beyond a few instances of simple addition. They are presented in the 'workshops' which you can skip if you wish. I have also placed 'Key Points to Remember' after each section on science. You can use them to easily compare the modern discoveries with the ancient descriptions.

This book leads you through a journey of discovery across numerous revelations given by ancient Yogis and Israelites who shared many beliefs. The descriptions they gave are impossible to know without the use of modern telescopes and computers. There are no known means by which these ancients could have gathered or guessed all this information. The quantity of legitimate facts is far too great: they have given a complete and accurate description of the *whole universe.*

Skeptics argue that our ancestors got it all wrong. The universe the ancients described is far too small to reflect reality.

But the truth is different.

Here is a preview of the astonishing worldview of the ancient Yogis: These amazing, delightful individuals didn't espouse a 'geocentric' world, one in which our planet Earth is the center of the universe, where the Sun revolves around the Earth. Neither did they support a 'heliocentric' world, one in which our Sun is the center of the universe. Instead, they believed the universe consists of limitless space where the notions of 'up,' 'down,' and 'center' are relative. They actually *state* this. The universe has no center, they explained. Aptly, then, they named our universe "Infinite Space" – *Param Akasha* or *Maha Akasha.*

Moreover, the Yogis described this great space as populated with innumerable star systems called *brahmandas* or 'cosmic eggs.' Externally, they are bubble-shaped, like a ball. They comprise of 'luminaries,' that is, stars and planets. Inside, many cosmic eggs have an immense, revolving disk of stars. Our Sun is a very small body floating within one of those starry disks, within one of those cosmic eggs, which in turn is but one of innumerable similar star systems floating in limitless space.

This grand description of the universe corresponds exactly with modern science. The cosmic eggs of the Yogis turn out to be none other than the galaxies discovered by scientists!

And these are just a few of the stunning new convergences. They constitute some of the most surprising and paradigm-breaking discoveries of recent times.

Most previous discoveries, though impressive, were different. They revealed the remarkable skills and expertise some ancients possessed in fields such as surgery and engineering. For instance, in 2500 BC ancient Egyptians had constructed magnificent pyramids. The Great Pyramid of Giza rose 146 meters – nearly 50 stories high. Amongst other wonders, its base is an almost perfect square and its north-south east-west orientation is accurate to a mean error of less than 1 degree.[6] Even today, it is still not fully understood how the pyramid was erected.

Similarly, about 600 BC, ancient Greeks dug a freshwater tunnel through solid limestone beneath a mountain on the Island of Samos. The tunnel was 1,036 meters long, 2 meters high, and 2 meters wide.[7] Extraordinarily, two teams began digging with hammers and chisels at opposite ends of the mountain, and met very much at the center. Scientists are still debating how they accomplished this marvel.

To the East, in India around 2600 BC, ancient Harrapans constructed grand cities such as Dholavira and Mohenjo-Daro. These metropolises sported two-story buildings, drainage systems, granaries, public baths, and stadiums. Each house had its own water well, bathroom, and lavatory with sewage running two meters beneath the ground through earthenware pipes. This was millennia before the rise of the Roman Empire![8] The Indians were also brilliant metallurgists who created magnificent steel Europeans could not match till the 1800s. An iron pillar from an ancient Hindu temple has not rusted even after 1700 years.[9] Scientists today still wonder at its pristine condition. Indians, as early as 1000 BC, were the first to inoculate against smallpox, saving the lives of millions of people who would otherwise have died from the infectious disease.[10] The English doctor Edward Jenner introduced the smallpox vaccine to Britain hundreds of years later in 1798. Indians were also pioneers of plastic surgery, Sushruta having successfully developed rhinoplasty around 400 BC.[11]

This was just a short list of the achievements of ancients around the world. Nevertheless, though extraordinary for their times, the feats were not intrinsically impossible. The required skills could be acquired through intelligence, astute observation, and lots of practice. They were not miraculous. Neither were they of the same complexity as achievements of the modern world. Supercomputers, space telescopes and satellites, nuclear technology, particle colliders, brain surgery, gene splicing, mapping the human genome, relativity theory, quantum theory, and so much more are all well beyond the achievements of those ancient people.

The point I am making is this: It is only through these very complex modern instruments and theories available today that we have been able to derive our detailed understanding of the cosmos. Without these tools, such knowledge is impossible. Similarly, without the same instruments at their disposal, it was impossible for ancient inventors and engineers to derive the same information, however intelligent they may have been. Yet, other people during those very same eras – individuals who weren't inventors, engineers, or physicians – clearly did derive the same information. It was an *absolutely impossible achievement.*

These exceptional individuals were the Yogis and Israelites. Unassuming people, they were often ascetics and recluses wearing nothing but a loincloth, sitting on mountains or river banks, far from towns or cities, and immersed in prayer or meditation.

Their detailed and authentic descriptions of the universe demonstrate the existence of a deeper, spiritual universe or God. By connecting to it, and without needing today's complex instruments, those souls could also connect with our physical world and describe it with stunning accuracy.

GENUINE PROOF FOR GOD

FIRST I WOULD LIKE TO CLARIFY what I mean by 'God.' I use this term throughout the book in a purely generic sense. It encompasses all spiritual beliefs – whatever one may call the Supreme Entity – God, Energy, Omnipotent Power, Absolute Being, Deity, Numen, Prime Mover, Creator, Universal Psyche, World Spirit, Life Force, Guardian Spirit, Divine Nature or any other concept indicating something wholesome and transcending the physical world.

What, then, constitutes evidence for this 'God'? The complexity of the DNA molecule? The blossoming of a rose in the morning? The fine tuning of the constants of nature? Do these prove the existence of a Grand Designer? Or do they prove we're living in one of infinite universes, and by necessity of chance, at least one of those infinite universes would have the characteristics we see in ours? We do not see God physically with our eyes and senses. We do not see him sitting on a cloud managing the workings of the world. We do not hear his words thundering from the sky. But many claim to feel his presence. Others claim to have experienced a miracle. Yet others claim to have had an 'out of body experience' or 'near death experience' or to have seen a 'tunnel of light.'[12] For these individuals, the event is a powerful, life-transforming experience, and in my opinion, a legitimate one. Thousands of people have had similar experiences across millennia. Surely, all these people can't be lying? What, then, about the experiences of those who wrote scripture? Do their words carry credibility, too?

This is the crux of the issue. Most of us haven't seen a star up-close. Yet, when scientists tell us stars are just like our Sun, only far away, we take their word for it. We haven't seen an electron. But when scientists tell us electricity is the flow of electrons, we take their word for it. When a doctor gives us information about our health, we take her word for it. We take the word of these people because we regard them as credible sources.

But the case is a little different with scripture. Since the claims of parchment are far more extraordinary than those of the above professions, some are skeptical. It was historically remote individuals who first taught us God exists. Who were the ancient saints, sages, and prophets? Were they fictitious? Who were the witnesses? Were they truthful and intelligent? Who were the authors? Were they gullible village folk duped by skillful conmen? Certainly, some of those ancient teachers convinced thousands of people of their sincerity and became the founders of the world's great Faiths. But millennia have passed. We live in a scientific age. Can we still take their word for it? They surely claimed to have seen God and experienced him in a direct way. Some, indeed, claimed to be sent by God, and more astoundingly, some claimed to *be* God. These were extraordinary claims and caution is understandable.

Today, even assuming the saints and authors were intelligent and honest, how can you know for sure they weren't schizophrenic, hallucinogenic, deluded, or anything else? This is the challenge of skeptics. They say there is no evidence at all, scientific or scriptural, for God's existence and that 'extraordinary claims' require extraordinary evidence.[13] In these times of scientific sophistication many are losing faith in God, spirituality, and scripture – beliefs and ancient works they feel are outdated, deficient, or simply wrong.

Have all your prayers been in vain? What will you say if you're asked about your beliefs? Will you have to tell those you love and care for that there is no one looking over them? That they have no soul? That they have no purpose in the world? That there is no heaven? That it may all be superstition? Speculation at best? That descriptions in ancient scripture don't correspond to reality? What will you say if you're asked: "What happens after I die?" "If God is one and truth is one, why are there many religions?" "Is the universe just a random event?" And there's another question that's often asked. Why is there pain and injustice in the world?

This is quite an emotional issue. Do you know someone who has suffered in his or her life? Have you ever been through a personal tragedy? Have you been through a terrible divorce? Have you ever witnessed a child's death? Do you know someone who had a miscarriage or stillbirth? Have you ever witnessed a natural disaster? Have you ever been the target of violence or bullying? Have you ever suffered an injustice? Have your prayers ever gone unanswered? If so, has any of the above ever caused you to wonder: "Does God really exist?" "Does he care?"

I recently received a letter from a lady called Emma living in New York. Her son, Daniel, had cancer. He was just ten. She visited her church every day and prayed for hours as her child received treatment for months. Her whole community prayed for him, too. But Daniel's condition worsened. Beset by anxiety and depression, she became dependent on prescription drugs.

At the hospital, Daniel would hug her and cry. "Mommy," he would say choking, "I don't want to die. Will God cure me? Is he listening to our prayers?" "Of-course he's listening," she would assure him. "You're going to be fine." But his condition continued to deteriorate. His body did not respond to treatment. One night, Emma received a call from the hospital. Daniel had passed on in his sleep.

Devastated, she sobbed for weeks. "Why did God do this to Daniel? Why did he do this to both of us? Does he care? Why didn't he answer our prayers? Does God even exist?"

She stopped going to church. She threw every spiritual motif she had out of her home. She cleared her altar. Taking to alcohol, she turned it into a bar. She tried to drink away her sorrow.

Some time later, her friend Sophia visited and gave her an earlier publication of this book *God Is Real*. Reluctantly, Emma started reading. However, to her own surprise, she couldn't put the book down! Reading through each chapter, her faith in the Bible and God was rejuvenated. "Though I lost Daniel," she wrote, "I'm now convinced that God exists, that the Bible is true, and that God loves Daniel and me. He loves us all. Daniel is waiting for me in a better place. If I had not read your book, I might even have taken my own life. Your book saved me. I thank my friend Sophia from the bottom of my heart for making me read it. And I thank you, too. Your book is truly a blessing."

Today, the evidence for God has become *objective*. You have it in your palms right now. It can be demonstrated to others. Even skeptics. It has been published in three mainstream science journals. Extraordinary evidence has arrived.

As has science, spirituality has come of age. And both are converging swiftly on numerous fronts. Due to psychological illness or imbalance, it is possible people may experience grandiose visions and hear voices in their heads. However, to experience joy and describe correctly the universe from A to Z aren't symptoms of illness or delusion. They are characteristics of divine minds.

Some scholars, on the contrary, would like us to believe that descriptions of the universe in the Bible and Yoga Literature are speculation. As these ancient people wandered about, other cultures exchanged material with them. One upon another, they say, more speculation was added and compiled into 'scripture.' Today, people like you and me take them to be spiritually revealed.[14]

You should know, however, that the ancient Yogis clearly stated they didn't acquire this knowledge through thinking, philosophy, or speculation. They received it through spiritual revelation. They weren't thinkers or philosophers masquerading as spiritual people. They were spiritual people showing us their souls.

Indeed, the hundreds of correspondences in the Bible and ancient Yoga Literature cannot have arisen through thinking or speculation. Even the greatest titans of speculation and intellectual pursuit such as Plato, Ptolomy, Aristotle, Galileo, and Newton *combined* couldn't derive all this knowledge. In fact, however acute your intellect may be, this knowledge of our universe is *impossible* to glean without the use of sophisticated mathematics together with powerful modern instruments. Its presence in ancient spiritual literature therefore demands *another* explanation.

The only rational and remaining explanation is a *spiritual* one. Indeed, it is the one given by the ancient sages and yogis themselves. Most importantly, the same spiritual path that led them to discover our universe and describe it in wonderful detail, also led them to discover God. When they said "God exists and loves you," *they spoke from direct spiritual experience.*

Let me address some other issues, too. Are these 100 convergences a form of 'numerology' – taking an *unexplained* ancient number and then trying to find a geological or galactic event that might coincide with it? Not at all. I have not reverse-engineered anything. The ancient Yogis gave all the information we need. They described vast numbers along with details of their accompanying geological or galactic events. They explained both the event and the timeframe in unambiguous, exact terms. There is no speculation involved in their interpretation. This is the beauty of these convergences. Neither is it 'cherry picking' – choosing from a vast array of options the ones that best fit modern science. Firstly, there is no vast array of options from which to choose a best fit. The ancient descriptions presented here are for the most part the *only* ones that exist. And the most powerful of these are the numerical ones.[15]

Numerical convergences are extremely difficult to strike by chance. For instance, the Yogis gave a very accurate timeline for many geological events including a global extinction and flood. Through sheer fantasy or ignorant guesswork, they could have given 4,000 years, 10,000 years, 15 million years, 89 trillion years or any of an infinite choice of timelines – any you may care to imagine. Therefore, their stating the correct answer of 429-120 million years ago out of this infinite choice of answers two millennia ago and striking bull's-eye by chance is simply impossible. And there isn't just one correct timeline. There are others that also converge with scientific discovery. In all, *nineteen* numerical bull's-eyes. What are the chances of that? To give an analogy, the chances are as improbable as a hurricane blowing through a scrap yard and assembling a ready-for-launch space shuttle! It's just impossible.

Nevertheless, I desist from presenting these convergences as *100 percent* proof for God's existence. It can never be 100 percent proven, nor disproven. By definition, God is all-transcendental, and beyond anything we can comprehend or measure with our human minds and scientific experiments. 100 percent proof for God's existence exists on the spiritual plane, and must come from within you. Why? Because that is where God resides. Nevertheless, the convergences do constitute 100 percent *genuine evidence* for God's existence. And if one is practical, they prove beyond 99.9 percent certainty that God exists.

The descriptions of the universe in ancient literature are valid and accurate. They weren't derived using modern instruments and you have seen that speculation alone, even by titans, can describe nothing close to reality. Logical thinking is not enough. This means the ancient descriptions *must* be spiritually revealed.

HABITUAL SKEPTICS

THE PAST SEVERAL YEARS HAVE seen a swarm of books by atheists who declare that there is not an iota of scientific evidence in support of spirituality. If there were, they claim, it is hard to see why any of the religions would want to shun such confirmation of their beliefs.[16]

Though, as the new convergences demonstrate, there is immense such evidence in the Bible and Yoga Literature, their challenge is misconceived. Which of the world's ancient spiritual teachers ever claimed that God is within the realm of experimental confirmation? Which spiritual beacon claimed that God would be visible through telescopes and microscopes, or derivable through a formula? In fact, these great spiritual guides emphasized that spiritual matters are transcendental and within the realm of experience alone.

Another argument by skeptics claims that Darwin's Theory of Evolution, or some versions of it, show that there is "almost certainly no God."[17]

"Almost," they state. Even after writing hundreds of pages denouncing religion and proclaiming 'no God,' it seems they are not fully convinced about it themselves! Indeed, the brilliant British scientist Stephen Hawking agrees that "God may exist."[18] Honest scientists are aware that their field can never procure 100 percent proof of God's existence nor of his non-existence, because God, by definition, exists beyond the material universe of space, time, and matter. Science can only investigate the natural universe. These are its limits. As a whale is mighty in the sea, but crippled upon land, so science is prodigious within the realm of physical experimentation, but powerless before the spiritual.

Compare this to the world's ancient spiritual mentors who were 100 percent *sure* of God's existence. This is because they spoke from direct experience.

Here are a few friendly words of advice to skeptics: you need to draw the line somewhere, or to at least respect the decision of the faithful to do so.

Is there any end to doubting?

Consider this: What *would* entrenched skeptics fully endorse as 100 percent proof of God's existence? There is nothing they can endorse fully. Because even if God was to appear before them upon a cloud in all his glory, they could easily doubt him and say, "Prove to us you are not an advanced extraterrestrial. Prove to us you are not an apparition. Prove to us that there is no life form higher than you. Prove to us that you are not some sort of illusion. Prove to us that you are eternal. Finally, prove to us that your proof is genuine and not a trick... ."

This is why the Bible advises, "Be *still,* and know that I am God" (Psalms 46:10) and the Yoga Literature expounds "As a turbulent stream will not reflect an image clearly, an unsteady mind cannot see the Light of God."

There is no end to doubting. You can find ways to doubt even the strongest proof. It becomes a habit, sometimes a self-defeating one. Doubting has a rightful place in the realm of scientific research, but not in matters of the transcendental, which is the realm of spiritual experience. No person can legitimately challenge the discoveries of science without having thorough knowledge and expertise of the subject. No person can legitimately challenge the logic of mathematical theorems without having advanced knowledge of them, either. Similarly, no person can legitimately challenge the assertions of spiritual and mystical discovery without having a personal and thorough experience of them as well.

Yet, some atheist scientists insist that all people must approach the "question" of God their way alone – that is, the scientific way – even though spirituality's greatest teachers have described spiritual matters as transcendental.

As an atom cannot be fathomed using hammers and pliers but requires particle accelerators and supercomputers, similarly, the spiritual realm is too subtle to be fathomed even with particle accelerators and supercomputers. It can only be fathomed through Faith, Prayer, and Yoga. But with doggedness, these scientists refuse to approach spiritual matters the transcendental way. If only they had the inquisitiveness to explore spirituality with an open, prayerful and meditative mind, they would begin to experience it for themselves, within themselves, and enjoy such spiritual growth that, who knows, they themselves might become 'saviors' one day… .

There is only one way to stop doubting: That is to start *trusting* – not everyone of-course, but at least those who are caring, sincere, and walk the talk. If they can find no person who satisfactorily meets their standards, skeptics need to open their hearts and minds and take a deep look at the new convergences of the Bible, ancient Yoga Literature, and modern science. They do not need to look anywhere else for evidence of God's existence: these ancient passages are filled with spectacular scientific Truths that reveal the wisdom, depth, and knowledge of their ancient inspirers.

SECRETIVE SAGES

WHY HAS SO MUCH SCIENTIFIC TRUTH within the Bible and Yoga Literature gone unnoticed for so long?

The ancient inspirers of these scriptures had great reverence for knowledge, be it about Self, God, or the Universe. It was therefore the norm in those ancient times to reveal knowledge only to those who genuinely aspired to 'walk the talk.' All knowledge comes from God. It's holy. It's sacred. It's eternal. Knowledge isn't for entertainment, but action. It's the path and it's the goal. It's the means and it's the end. This was their belief. Sacred knowledge was to be bequeathed only to those who genuinely aspired to learn. So they kept it secret and codified. They forestalled access to their texts by using every tool they could: parables, imagery, symbols, similes, allegories, metaphors, epithets, and abstractions.[19] The texts are deliberately baffling. The Bible and Yoga Literature are cryptic.

How old is this literature? The documents containing the cosmic descriptions are truly ancient. One – *The Rig Veda* – is considered to be amongst the oldest extant literature of humankind. It dates back at least 3500 years, or 1500 BC. For millennia it was customary for Yogi students to completely memorize what they were taught by their teachers. Scripture was transmitted through an oral tradition. To facilitate this, the early teachers arranged and composed their teachings into metrically attuned verses in Sanskrit. Various metrical formats can be found in the vast majority of ancient Yoga Literature. UNESCO declared the ancient tradition of the Rig Veda 'A Masterpiece of the Oral and Intangible Heritage of Humanity' in its Proclamation in 2003.[20]

Cosmic descriptions can also be found in the literature of various later works called the *Puranas*. Other remarkable passages are encountered in the *Pancharatra*, *Mahabharata*, *Ramayana,* and *Yoga Vasishta*. More can be discovered in the *Yoga Sutras* of Patanjali and various *Upanishads*. Startling passages also emerge from the *Vedras* and *Vachanamrutam* texts that date back to the early nineteenth century. All these works along with many others constitute the teachings of the ancient Yogis.

Dating the more ancient Yoga texts accurately, however, has proven elusive. The Rig Veda, for instance, may actually be as old as 1900 BC or even 2500 BC.[21] Other works are somewhat later and range between 1000 BC to 1000 AD. Certainly, all predate the scientific era by many, many centuries. The Bible is similarly ancient and dates back to about 1000 BC with the New Testament originating nearly 2,000 years ago.

Let us take a brief look at the content of these texts, for instance, the Rig Veda. On the surface, it seems to be a lengthy book describing mundane objects such as cattle, horses, chariots, battles, crops, the weather, Sun, Moon, and day and night. Yet its adherents made heroic efforts to memorize this text, passing it from generation to generation, without losing a single syllable even after four thousand years!

Why did they do so much to preserve these texts? What was so valuable about them?

The answer lies in understanding that they aren't, as skeptics like to assume, a compilation of mythical beliefs about nature and the weather.

They are *mystical* revelations concerning God, creation, and the universe.

The descriptions of the weather are playful allegories of their profound spiritual experiences. It's unfortunate that many scholars ignore this, even though the ancient Yogis themselves hint at the cryptic nature of their statements three times in the book itself.

Here are relevant passages from the Bible and Yoga Literature that reveal their deliberately enigmatic nature. (Non-English words in parentheses are Sanskrit.)

Without a parable he [Jesus] didn't speak to them;
but privately to his own disciples he explained everything.

Bible, Mark 4:34

Then his disciples asked him,
"What does this parable mean?"
He said, "To you it is given to know
the mysteries of the Kingdom of God,
but to the rest in parables;
that 'seeing they may not see,
and hearing they may not understand.'

Bible, Luke 8:9-10

In them the prophecy of Isaiah is fulfilled, which says,
'By hearing you will hear, and will in no way understand;
Seeing you will see, and will in no way perceive.

Bible, Matthew 13:14-15

To you I shall now declare this most secret knowledge,
having known which,
you shall be free from the pangs of this world.
Of sciences, it is king; of secrets, it is king.[22]

Bhagavad Gita 9:1-2

If anyone amongst all these monks and lay disciples
understands this talk,
immense good will come to their soul.
This talk is not of the type
to give before a general congregation.

Vachanamruta, Gadhada II.13

That person who is in the right eye,
he is called Indha ['the Kindler'],
and him who is Indha they call indeed *Indra* cryptically;
for the divinities love what is cryptic,
and dislike what is evident.[23]

Brihadaranyaka Upanishad 4.2.2; Shatapatha Brahmana 6:1.1.2.11;
Aitareya Upanishad 1:3.14; Aitareya Brahmana 3:33 end, 7:30 end.

All the divinities have taken their seats
upon the supreme heaven,
that is, the imperishable knowledge of the Veda.

What will he who does not know this do with the Veda?
But those who do know are Perfect.

Rig Veda Samhita 1.164.39

By its many levels of meaning,
the Vedas mislead those who are dulled by ritual verses.

Bhagavata Purana 10.87.36

There are four types of speech.
Three of them are deposited in secret
and indicate no meaning.
[But] those wise brahmanas [Yogis] know them.

Rig Veda Samhita 1.164.45

O Sage who is wise,
I address these soliciting mysterious
[or secret] poems.

Rig Veda Samhita 4.3.16

From the above, it is clear that the inspirers of the Bible and ancient Yoga Literature intentionally spoke cryptically and revealed the hidden meaning of their message only to their closest.

Accordingly, couched within their mystical descriptions of God, the ancient teachers also described global geological events, immense cosmic structures, and the entire universe using symbols and abstractions. They used broad terms like earth, water, light (or fire), gas (or wind), and space. They also used common objects such as eggs, their shell and shape, or trees, gardens, groves, fruits, forests, lotus flowers, creeper plants, water wells, mountains, the

Sun, Moon, sky, ocean, whirlpools, salt, pots, needle holes, iron, gold, dust, horses, chariots, constellations, thunderclaps, lightning, fortresses, human beings, demons, angels, birth and death, creation and destruction, day and night, light and darkness. Due to the use of so many metaphors and abstractions, it was inevitable their descriptions of the world would convey little to the uninitiated. Said the ancient Yogi Vasishta:

"Things that are inaccessible
to the likes of you in experience ... though they exist,
seem inconsistent when spoken of by the likes of me."

Yoga Vasishta 6.2.59. 38

The confusion and misapprehension was compounded by the fact that scientists didn't know much about our universe until the 1950s. Fortunately, in the past few decades, science has made great leaps. And a comparison of the ancient with the modern reveals many convergences. When you examine closely the ancient descriptions of the universe, you find them studded with the same dazzling discoveries of modern science.

Indeed, it's interesting that science writers also describe the universe using metaphors and abstractions. For instance, they often describe galaxies as 'giant pinwheels' in space. One galaxy is actually named the 'Pinwheel Galaxy.' (Figure 3.7)

Another familiar term is 'black hole.' This refers to an extremely dense, gravitating object that doesn't let light escape from it. However, this extraordinary meaning would only be known to those who have learnt about it. To others it could mean something as ordinary as a hole in the ground, or a cave, or tunnel.

One of the most famous metaphors used by science is possibly the 'Milky Way.' A person without any knowledge of this word might think it referred to a particular candy bar or a river flowing with milk. An informed individual would know that it refers to the sparkling band of visible stars in the night sky, and in a larger context, to our entire Galaxy.

It's not unusual, then, that the ancients used metaphors, too. Today, in the light of recent discoveries, these ancient descriptions make a lot of sense and radiate an elegant and accurate picture of our universe. The passages sound like a symphony. The cosmic landscape they paint is magnificent and coherent. Most importantly, the time scales of modern cosmology agree closely.

How could the Yogis and Israelites get so much right?

OMNISCIENT YOGIS – AND *YOU*

PARAPSYCHOLOGY, OR *PSI*, IS AN AREA of research that attracted much attention in the 70s and 80s. It was the age of international espionage. There are claims that the United States and Russian governments invested large sums of money in research and development of *psi* or ESP – extra sensory perception. If it truly existed, and if they could harness it, the advantages might be significant. Whatever the truth of these claims, some institutes and universities do study ESP today. Their results have been positive but controversial.[24]

Generally, ESP is the ability to perceive hidden things from a distance using nothing but one's mind and consciousness. These abilities are sometimes called clairvoyance, remote viewing, remote listening, remote touching, and so on. Such abilities are extraordinary.

Yoga, however, is a discipline that far surpasses clairvoyance. When practised in its eight-fold holistic form known as 'Ashtanga Yoga' (which is distinct from the exercise regime it's usually associated with), yoga is the ultimate tool to cultivate and channelize your conscious energy.

Ancient Yogis explained you possess more than your five senses of sight, sound, smell, taste, and touch. You have a sixth sense – the mind.[25] It is much subtler than the physical senses and is more than an information processing unit. Just as your bodily senses can be enhanced through proper training, so too can your mind. Unlike the bodily senses, however, your mind has virtually no limits. When quieted and trained, it can send and receive information from any source in the universe, regardless of how far the object may be.

After knowledge of the Self is attained [through yoga],
then intuitive hearing, feeling, seeing, tasting and smelling,
omnipotence, and omniscience come into being.

Yoga Sutra 3.35, 48

The dominion of the Yogi's mind
extends from the supreme particle
to the supremely-great.

Yoga Sutra 1.40

Knowledge of subtle, obstructed and far-away things
arises from yoga.

OMNISCIENT YOGIS – AND YOU

Yoga Sutra 3.24

The disciple asked:
What you saw then in your ... consciousness – was it seen by
you while you were staying in one place or while moving about?

The Yogi replied:
I was neither essentially stationed in one place,
nor was I essentially mobile.
Thus I saw this within my own self here.

Yoga Vasishta 6.2.62.1-3

For people like me,
this [knowledge] is directly perceivable,
not arrived at by speculation.

Yoga Vasishta 6.2.128.1, 4

Once, having learned what you need to know,
you come to possess immaculate vision
of the past, present, and future,
then you shall perceive them
[the multitude of worlds] directly.

Yoga Vasishta 6.2.176.1-6, 21, 25

The steadfast perceive everything with their eye
perfected through yoga.

Bhagavata Purana 3.11.13-17

[I] can see infinite millions
of Cosmic Eggs [Galaxies]
as easily as a drop of water in my palm.

Vachanamruta, Gadhada II.53

This is the power of Ashtanga Yoga practiced by the ancient Yogis!
It guides you step-by-step through the process of training your
mind and releasing the power of your consciousness. When practiced regularly, it can unleash unlimited potential. When perfected,
the whole universe will be revealed to you. You don't have to
travel anywhere to get this knowledge. It surges from within you.
You experience the whole cosmos right where you're sitting,
standing, walking, or resting.

For this exquisite knowledge to dawn, your mind should become not just quiet, but silent. When there is absolutely no mental
noise, the subtlest sounds and farthest sights of the universe can be

heard and seen. The information you receive, in whatever amount, nurtures the development of your mind, body, and soul, in fact your entire life, your actions, and your destiny. Yoga therefore leads to joy, enlightenment, and empowerment. Using yoga wisely, you can expand and grow yourself – personally, financially, and spiritually – beyond your wildest dreams!

But there are further limits, still. For those who desire to explore the uttermost limits of their powers, continued practice of Ashtanga Yoga bestows entry into a spiritual world that transcends and trumps the senses. Yoga is the bridge to that imponderable and intangible world where time does not exist as you know it; where space does not isolate two people; where plurality blends into unity. Here, one attains a direct experience of God. It is ineffable, indescribable. The Yogis used only three words – Truth (*sat*), Consciousness (*chit*), and Bliss (*ananda*) – to relate the glorious experience.

Yoga connects you directly to all knowledge and all truths. The whole universe is interconnected. No object, no person or creature, no time, past, present or future, no emotion – anger, depression or love – no beliefs of the great Faiths, and no values of society can be isolated from one another. Everything connects with everything else. No one and nothing is dispensable. All are important, all is holy, and all is whole. This is the eternal truth espoused by Yogis since millennia. This is the potency of Yoga.

It isn't made up. It isn't speculation. It isn't thinking. It's direct experience.

During my time in India, I learned the ancient art of Yoga and Meditation from a Grand Master and practiced it fives times a day for decades. This dedicated practice led me to an inner awakening that revealed the spiritual oneness of all people and all great spiritual traditions. It also led to profound peace and joy. With a little practice, you can learn and experience it, too.

YOGA HUGS ALL FAITHS

PERHAPS MORE THAN ANY OTHER alternative lifestyle, yoga is proving effective and beneficial. Why is this? Because it's holistic. It's about body, mind, soul, and God. It integrates all four. It doesn't advise you to pursue one at the expense of the other.

Not only does yoga encourage this balanced approach, it also shows you how it can be easily nurtured: Through a Yogic lifestyle. This includes the practice of stretching postures, breathing exercises, and meditations. Doing just a little of these can enhance your health, state of mind, and powers of intuition enormously. Your intuition can become so sharp, you can know instinctively whether doing something will be good for you or not. This helps you make better choices and it influences your destiny. Your innermost dreams can be realized. Success can be yours.

There are many other benefits, too. Yoga can reduce stress, help quit smoking, alcohol, and drugs. It's useful in pain management. It's great for anger management. It makes you more personable, friendly, and empathetic. It helps you forgive. It calms you down. It makes you peaceful. The list of benefits goes on almost forever.

If you take care of your body and mind, they will take care of you. Similarly, the world is part of you too, say the Yogis. Take care of it, and it will take care of you. Respect the cosmos. Protect the environment. Revere nature. Love life. Love peace. As you shall sow, so shall you reap.

How can all this be done? Again, through yoga! Yoga connects you to the cosmos, and it responds. Things begin to take shape. You begin to realize your special purpose in the world. Events happen that take you in profoundly new directions. 'Coincidences' you can't explain begin to occur. You meet new people who help you towards your newfound goal. Information comes your way that catapults you ahead. In fact, so much begins to happen, you can barely keep up. This is the wonderful difference yoga can make to your life and those around you.

Don't shortchange yourself. Fulfill your purpose. It's there for you to achieve. But first you must make a pilgrimage to your center stage, your inner self, your soul. That is where success begins and also where it culminates.

Having said all this about Yoga, however, you should know that it is *not* itself a religion. It is spirituality in its most open and malleable form. It's a tool, an instrument. It showers benefits on anyone who uses it, whichever spiritual background they may belong to. It nourishes your body, mind, and soul. It takes you towards better health and God in a single sweep.

You can't help but experience something spiritual when you practice yoga. Indeed, the discoveries of this book are due to the practice of yoga. The same discoveries can be made by you, whatever your spiritual background or leanings, providing you practice 'Yogic' principles. And you don't have to call it yoga to practice it. The benefits are not tied to its name but its implementation.

Moreover, yoga encourages you to practice whichever persuasion of thought you wish. It doesn't require you to reject the doctrines of your creed. In fact, the spiritual doctrines of all traditions are important because they were disseminated by those who spoke from experience. However, the truth of a doctrine is not justification for denying seekers their own direct experience of the Divine. Yogic meditation or contemplation is about going beyond thought and theory into personal experience, however minimal. It's about going deeper than concepts, into Reality, however unfathomable. Meditation offers the seeker an opportunity to glimpse his or her own soul and the Sovereign Spirit residing within.

Thoughts take you into the past or future. They are usually about desires, tribulations, and anxieties that are gone or yet uncertain of arrival. They have no real use and consume your time and energy. The Bible recognizes this wastefulness and recommends the fundamentals of meditation.

In the Sermon on the Mount, Jesus advised the congregations to shun their anxieties of the past and future, and to live in the present. "Therefore don't be anxious, saying, 'What will we eat?', 'What will we drink?' or, 'With what will we be clothed?' ... But seek first God's Kingdom ... ." (Matthew 6:31-34) He taught people to seek this kingdom of God *within.* "The Kingdom of God doesn't come with observation; neither will they say, 'Look, here!' or, 'Look, there!' for behold, the Kingdom of God is within you." (Luke 17:21) These are the basic principles of yoga! God, said St. Catherine of Siena in the 4th century, is the center of your soul.

So close is the Lord, yet as far as the stars if one doesn't delve within.

It's an experience that transcends all words and concepts. All languages ancient and modern collapse before the immeasurable and ineffable experience of the soul and God. Say the ancient Yogis, "From where all words, along with the mind, turn away unable to reach it."[26] Meditation connects you directly to your inner spiritual core. As the 19th century French Jesuit Pierre Teilhard de Chardin famously said, "We are not human beings having a spiritual experience, but spiritual beings having a human experience."

All the ancient teachers of the world's great religions invite you to discover your true Self and untapped abilities. You are as a rose bud, closed, but laden with color and fragrance. A little light from the Sun is all that is required to awaken you. The goal of yoga is, therefore, to take you from bud to flower, from physical existence to spiritual essence.

Accomplished Yogis (males) and Yoginis (females) come from all religious backgrounds and all walks of life. From monks and nuns, kings and queens, sciences and arts, poor and rich, old and young, strong and athletic, frail and disabled. These Yogis (I will use this term henceforth to include Yoginis) can have various levels of achievement. Some are beginners, some are masters, some are giants. Most importantly, the scope and subject of their experiences will depend on the direction and focus of their meditation. Some Yogis will have had experiences and glimpses of their soul and God. Others will have had the same of our Galaxy and universe. Yet others will have had both. Most will have had neither, but will have experienced profound peace. Of all, this is by far the most important.

Interestingly, in a recent survey, 70 percent of Americans with a religious affiliation said they believe that there isn't only one way to God.[27] The faithful from other traditions can reach God, too. This is a welcome signal indicating the growing awareness of the legitimacy of other spiritual Faiths. It's a move away from rigid fanaticism to the honest acceptance that other spiritual traditions also teach good things.

Details of doctrine aren't important to many people. Most will ask just two questions: 1. Do you believe in God? 2. Do you believe in treating others as you wish them to treat you? This is basic spirituality and ethics. It's not unique to the Bible or Yoga Literature. The differences between the world's major Faiths are mostly of terminology and culture. The cosmology shared by the ancient Yogis and Israelites support this view.

For far too long, religious beliefs have divided and isolated the world's Faiths. Now, the correspondences between science and spirituality and between various ancient traditions are pulling them together. Religious 'exclusivism' – the belief that one's own religion is the only true religion and that all others are in error – is not supported by impartial, objective studies. Indeed, the opposite is established: spiritual inclusivism and universalism. We are all truly climbing the same proverbial mountain from different sides.

Additionally, the ever-increasing popularity of yoga is gradually *knitting* people together. Indeed, yoga *means* 'union.' All these convergences foster mutual admiration between science, spirituality, and its many Faiths.

In several ways this new synthesis and integration has already begun by some spiritual groups reaching across the aisle to other Faiths. I also reached out to other communities and compared two seemingly disparate traditions – the Bible of the West and the Yoga Literature of the East.

What I found blew me away: A convergence of East and West. The descriptions of creation and global extinction in Genesis are synopses of counterparts in ancient Yoga Literature that clearly converge with science. Necessarily, then, Genesis must also converge with science.

On the other hand, sadly, as we see a rise of religious fanaticism in some parts of the world, we also witness another brand of fundamentalism raising its ugly head. Atheistic fanaticism. Both are damaging to the future of our beautiful planet.

And both groups are profoundly mistaken.

SCIENCE AND SPIRITUALITY CONVERGE

IT IS SOMETIMES THOUGHT THAT SCIENCE and scientists in general are atheistic, denying there is a Deity who created the universe. This is a misperception. Many scientists of the highest repute have espoused belief in God and spirituality – together with their relevance in reaping knowledge of the universe.

In fact, a large portion of the scientific community has gone on record in the high-ranking science journal *Nature* stating their belief in a Deity.[28] In the 1997 landmark survey, American scientists were asked if they believed in a God to whom they could pray. 39.3 percent of them said *yes*. Researchers who conducted the study observed that a broader definition of God would have revealed an even higher percentage of believers.[29] Such a definition may have included belief in a God that created the universe and its laws, but left it to unfold automatically without ever intervening.

When such a large percentage of scientists affirm their belief in spirituality, it's a sign that the two disciplines don't necessarily collide. In fact, the new correspondences show they converge. They are merely different pathways to discovery. One outer, the other inner.

Modern and ancient people describe our Galaxy and universe according to their times and purposes. Scientists use pictures and mathematics. The ancients used metaphors and abstractions.

But was everything they said perfect? Does all of it correspond with science? From what I have described till now it may appear to you as though everything the Yogis said about our world is accurate. With all fairness, I must state that not all of their descriptions are unmarred. I believe it's objectionable to misguide people by telling partial truths, even for 'good' reasons. Only whole truths will stand the test of time. As such, you should know from the outset that some descriptions of the ancient Yogis just don't jibe. In all, about five percent of their discussions of the world remain mysterious.[30]

For instance, they correctly describe all the night stars and our Sun to be within a starry disk that revolves in a clockwise direction around an extremely minute but luminous center. They call this center the 'Meru' or sometimes, 'Mount Meru.'[31] This much is fine – fantastic, in fact. But there's a twist. In some passages the shape of this luminous Meru seems to be likened to the conical seed cup of a lotus flower.[32] (Figure 3.11, p. 119) Yet, other passages accurately describe the cosmic structure as spherical.

There are other puzzles. The ancients said it takes one 'year' (*samvatsara*) for the Sun to revolve around the starry disk. Scientists utilize the word 'year,' too. But it represents a 'galactic year.' It spans about 225 million Earth years. If it turns out that there is no similar explanation for the Sanskrit term, then this ancient description seems discordant with science.

Yet other passages say the night stars receive their light from the Sun and Moon, that the Moon is made of water and is the support of the entire world. Others say the Sun is the support of all the stars. Yet others say that the Sun absorbs moisture from the Earth and gives it to the Moon. In turn, the Moon passes it back down to Earth through tubes of air. The clouds, which are vessels of smoke, fire, and wind, retain these waters. Moreover, other passages state the Sun absorbs water from a celestial river in the sky. The rain that falls when there are no clouds in the sky are the waters of this river, shed by the Sun's rays.

On the other hand, there are beautiful passages that correctly state the Moon is just a ball of dull matter illuminated by the Sun. They even correctly state that eclipses of the Moon occur due to the Earth's shadow falling upon it.[33]

Again, the ancients correctly placed the Sun at the center of our solar system. But there seem to be problems with the details. These concern the distances between the Sun and the Earth, the orbits of the planets, their diameters, and the distances to the Pole star and other stars, and the central Meru around which they all revolve. For some curious reason, for instance, the ancients said the Moon has twice the diameter of the Sun. This doesn't concur even with what we plainly see in the sky. This strongly suggests the Yogis were using hyperbole while eulogizing the Moon. This may also be true for the other inaccurate descriptions. Nonetheless, the distances and dimensions as they stand seem plainly wrong.

Importantly, passages like these are peripheral and don't form the central core of the Yogis' worldview. Moreover, they may be ascribed to the exuberance of the Yogis while they worshipped, or to the unfathomable mysticism of their experiences. Whatever the answer, they seem inconsistent with modern science. All these enigmas comprise about five percent of the cosmic descriptions of the ancient Yogis.

More striking, though, is the fact that ninety-five percent of their Big Picture is *correct*.

Are the few inconsistencies important or trivial? Does their presence disprove the ninety-five percent of correct convergences that are *impossible* to know without the instruments of modern science? Are the inconsistencies simply the result of lost or fragmentary texts? Or could it be that they reflect the exuberance of the

Yogis during their moments of devotion? Or are they indicative the ancients used metaphors some of which we're still unfamiliar with?

No doubt, 'skeptics of the gaps' in ancient scripture will pounce on these mysteries as 'proof' that God doesn't exist. But they need to bear in mind that the ancient Yogis touched on a vast spectrum of very difficult subjects that range from our Oceans and Earth to the Sun, Galaxy, and Universe. And, for the most part, they spoke of them accurately. Skeptics should also remember that the worldview the Yogis opined was discovered by science only in the past fifty years using complex theories and state-of-the-art instruments. Therefore, legitimate knowledge drawing on so many disciplines in ancient times was absolutely impossible.

Consider this: Amongst the Greek thinkers, only a few such as Plato and Socrates believed the Earth is round.[34] And about the rest of the universe, these two knew next to nothing.

Indeed, as we saw earlier, titans of pure intellectual thought such as Plato, Aristotle, Ptolomy, Galileo, and Newton *combined* couldn't derive all the knowledge given by the ancient Yogis.

All this reflects the fact that ancient thinkers really didn't know much about our Earth at all, let alone the universe. We know today that this is because the Earth, and certainly the universe, are just too large to be understood with the naked eye. We need powerful instruments and mathematical formulae. These tools help us understand what's happening around us. Without them, our sensory perception is superficial and leads to incorrect conclusions. Logical thinking is insufficient.

The saga of worldviews proposed by ancient thinkers varies like a kaleidoscope. The great Greek philosopher Anaximander (610-546 BC) concluded the Earth is a cylinder surrounded by fire. Between the Earth and fire there is a curtain with holes in it. Light from the fire escapes through these holes and appears to us as stars. The eminent Italian philosopher Hippolytus (170-235 BC) concluded that the Earth was one of the two flat ends of a great pillar. Even the brilliant Greek philosopher Aristotle (384-322 BC) believed our Earth is the center of the universe and that the Sun, planets, and stars revolve around it, embedded in a series of transparent, crystalline spheres.

It might appear astonishing that our prized ancestors harbored these 'naive' ideas about the world. But we shouldn't forget that the scientific wisdom we possess today is the culmination of work accrued across centuries of history and discovery. In earlier days, those naive conclusions were derived through considerable thought and observation. Seeing was believing. Observation made things self-evident. The belief that the world is flat and the Sun revolves around the Earth had been a visible 'fact' demonstrated twice a day, since eons. Even the relatively modern Newton proposed that the universe revolves around our Sun.[35]

All these beliefs had a rational foundation. What those ideas truly display is not a lack of intelligence or thought, but how extremely problematic it is to grasp the nature of the cosmos without the use of modern instruments and mathematical theorems. The naked eye and the untrained mind can be devilishly deceiving.

If everything in the world was as obvious as it seems to the eye, Plato and others would have correctly resolved these issues millennia ago. Considering the great intellectual stature of all these individuals and their dismal failure to grasp the universe, it would be amazing if the ancient Yogis in their loincloths could describe even 2 percent of the universe correctly.

Therefore, getting 95 percent right is simply mind-blowing.

APPEARANCES CAN BE DECEIVING

THOUSANDS OF YEARS AGO, some people believed the Earth was flat. If you walked or sailed far enough, you could fall over the edge. Moreover, not only did they believe the Earth is the center of the solar system, they believed it's the center of the universe.

On the other hand, see how things were panning out in India. Ancient Yogis spoke almost as modern scientists. They themselves warned that appearances could be deceiving. Remarkably, they recommended the following training to student-Yogis who wanted to learn about the universe: along with the study of scripture, they should cultivate a keen intellect, astute observation, counting (mathematics), timing (using water clocks), and drawing (using diagrams).

It is not possible for any human being
to factually comprehend
the coming and going of the stars and planets

by using the naked eye.

Their movements should be understood
by discerning people after intelligent examination,
from scripture, inference,
direct perception
and demonstrable arguments.

The eye [observation], scripture, water [water clock],
drawing [diagrams], and counting [mathematics],
o best knowers of intelligence –
these five are the means
of investigating the host of stars, o priests.

Brahmanda Purana 1.2.24.150-152abcd

This is a truly commendable statement coming from an ancient Yogi. It is very much the method of science. It is clear the ancients respected science, encouraged it, and opined complementing it with spirituality. They recommended a balanced approach. This was their genuine spirit.

They weren't dogmatic. They weren't naive. They weren't bigoted. In fact, their minds were far more open to science than many skeptics' are to spirituality. The tables have turned. Today, it is skeptics who are usually chauvinistic and opinionated. Just as there are people who abuse spirituality, people who teach and do preposterous things in the name of religion, so too there are people who teach and do preposterous things in the name of science. But just as religion and spirituality do not belong to such hijackers, neither does science belong to its abductors. Those who teach that science proves there is no God are distorting science. Science has no jurisdiction over the immaterial, divine world. Moreover, in the world of faith, and according to the ancient Yogis, science is actually a tool to take one closer to God. Science is a form of worship, an exploration to understand as far as possible the mind and creation of God.

The ancient Yogis were pioneers of investigative techniques, both outer and inner. Their conclusions are stunning and counterintuitive: the outer universe that science studies today is but a microcosm, while the inner world is the *macro*cosm.

Humankind has a lot of exploring to do.

Before we move on to the really juicy core of this book, I would like to show you some excerpts concerning something I touched on earlier: The immense worldview of the Yogis. Below you will see what they believed about our Earth's shape and how our planet fitted into their cosmology.

In this great endless space
these cosmic eggs ... appear as an illusion ... .

What in [each] cosmic egg is the earthy part,
that is down, and [what is] otherwise is up.

For example, as for great ants standing
all over a spherical clod of earth
suspended in space,
their feet [despite their opposite locations]
are [reckoned] 'below'

and their backs are [reckoned] 'above'... .

This [earth] with its villages,
cities and mountains came into being ...
like a ripe walnut with its coat.

Yoga Vasishta 3.30.1-34

This was the worldview of the ancient Yogis. It's extraordinarily modern. In endless space, they said, there are innumerable cosmic eggs (galaxies). In these great worlds the notion of up and down is relative to where there are earthy structures, what we call 'planets.' Moving toward these is 'down' and away is 'up.' These earthy structures are suspended in space like clods of earth in the sky. Living beings move all over these structures as ants move over a suspended clod of earth. Our Earth, too, is populated with life all over it. Like a walnut, it's spherical.

This is simply beautiful!

Interestingly, the Bible contains a similar statement.

He [God] stretches out the north over empty space,
and hangs the earth on nothing.

Bible, Job 26:7

But hold your breath. These were just a prelude to the major convergences to follow.

They are real.

All the scientific descriptions in this book have been fact-checked and approved by scientists in each field.[36]

We will begin our trek at the deepest depths of our Earth's oceans. Thousands of years ago, could the Yogis have known what resides there?

Come, let us begin this humbling voyage.

WHAT THE ANCIENT YOGIS KNEW

VOLCANOES UNDER THE SEA

IT IS SURPRISING THAT FOUR DECADES after man landed on the Moon a quarter of a million miles away, scientists still know little about the seafloor located just a few miles beneath the ocean surface.

Why is this?

For starters, the most immediate challenge for researchers is the immense water depth separating ships from the seafloor. On average, the oceans are 12,000 feet deep, while the deepest ocean trench is located beneath 36,000 feet of water. This depth is roughly equivalent to the elevation at which modern aircraft cruise above the Earth.

Furthermore, humans are ill-equipped to handle the extreme conditions of the oceans. Water quickly absorbs the wavelengths of visible light, hindering basic observations. For example, at a depth of just 400 feet, darkness reduces visibility to essentially zero. Then, there is the problem of temperature. Without special diving gear, a diver quickly loses body heat to seawater, which can be extremely chilly. Furthermore, a diver without breathing apparatus needs to surface frequently for air.

The most formidable challenge, however, results from the increase of pressure with increasing depth in the ocean. The weight of water is so extreme it prevents even well-protected divers from descending to depths greater than about 350 feet. This is because the pressure increases rapidly with depth. Therefore, without a specially designed submarine, diving to 12,000 feet – the average depth of the oceans – is utterly impossible. The pressure there is a crushing two tonnes per square inch.

With such hurdles to overcome, seafloor exploration was slow and arduous. Scientists conducting the first expeditions and ship surveys in the 1870s incorrectly concluded that the seafloor is basically flat and muddy. It was not until the Second World War that the use of newly available sonar equipment led to the discovery of mountain ranges under the North Atlantic and Pacific Oceans. Close to 100 submarine mountains were charted – a dramatic contrast to the conclusions drawn in the late nineteenth century.

Later surveys, utilizing increasingly sophisticated equipment, revealed that the mountain ranges were part of a mountain chain some 35,000 miles long, with some peaks rising to more than 12,000 feet above the sea floor. The mountain chain branches to form a network around the entire Earth like the seams of a baseball. (Figure 1.1) Although hidden from sight, the mountain chain forms the largest geological feature on the planet.

The question arose: How did these mountains form? It was discovered that they were volcanic.

In fact, they are sites where hot lava originating deep in the Earth's mantle erupts from giant cracks in the Earth's crust. The erupting lava rapidly solidifies on the ocean floor when it comes into contact with the cold water. These enormous mountains mark the locations of ongoing eruptions where the volcanic rock that makes up oceanic crust is formed.

In 1977, scientists used a deep-sea research submarine, or submersible, to explore the sea floor near the Galapagos Islands in the

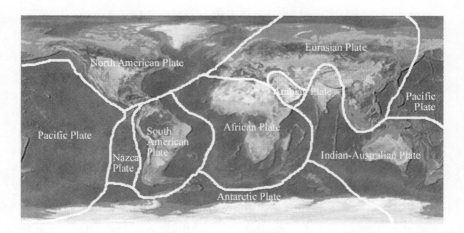

Fig 1.1. White lines show major locations of the mountain chain network found beneath all the oceans. Along this mountain chain are deep cracks in the Earth's crust that ooze lava, and where hydrothermal vents and large submarine volcanoes form.

Pacific Ocean. It was an epochal event. What the scientists saw stupefied them.

They discovered hydrothermal vents, geysers where boiling hot water spouts from chimney-like orifices on the sea floor. These vents have now been found all over the world, usually at depths greater than 1.5 miles. They commonly form on volcanoes that are a part of the submarine mountain chain.

The discovery of hydrothermal vents resolved an issue scientists were struggling with for years. It was known that salts have been eroding from minerals in the rocks on the continents for billions of years. The constant addition of salts to the ocean suggested that the concentration of salts in seawater should have risen.[37] But, this hadn't happened.

How could it be?

The riddle was resolved upon investigating the amount of salts present in fluids expelled from hydrothermal vents. The fluids were discovered to be depleted in salts. A range of salinities, measured using the concentration of sodium chloride, were found to be well below normal seawater salinity values, sometimes just five percent of normal concentrations.[38]

Where was this desalinated water coming from?

Curiously, the answer was from the ocean itself.

Hydrothermal fluids move through a conduit system, in which seawater is expelled at vents far from the sites where it entered. The water enters the system through cracks and tiny pores in the volcanic rock of the sea floor. The water descends deep into the crust, and at depths of 1–2 miles, circulates through heated rocks that reside above magma chambers containing molten rock. Here, the water is heated to supercritical conditions and, through various processes, becomes depleted of its salts.

The superheated salt-depleted fluid then rises up through cracks in the rock and exits the sea floor at vents. As in a siphon system, the exit of water from a vent at one end causes new water to be sucked in at the other.[39] It's as though the volcanic structures are drinking the ocean's water. (Figure 1.2)

Scientists estimate that all the water in the oceans is pulled through a hydrothermal system once every twenty million years. This process regulates the salt content of our oceans.[40]

The chloride-depleted water exiting the vents is not like bottled water, though. It's often dark and smoky in appearance, rich in sulfides and other dissolved minerals extracted from the hot rocks at depth. The dissolved minerals carried in the hydrothermal fluids precipitate around the vents, making them shine and glitter with metal sulfide minerals. Even a dusting of minute grains of gold has been found at some sites.[41]

In addition to the network of volcanic ridges circling the globe, there are also isolated patches of volcanism in the oceans. These sites sit above plumes of abnormally hot rock rising within the Earth's mantle. The areas at the Earth's surface above the plumes are called hotspots. Hotspots are areas of persistent volcanic activity. At

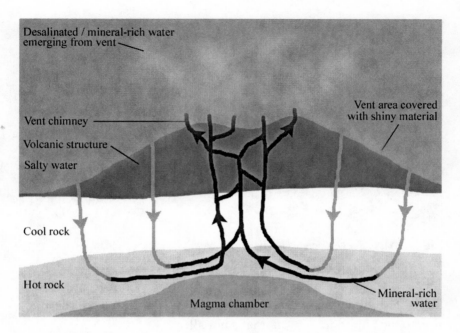

Fig 1.2. Schematic diagram of a typical hydrothermal system. Not to scale.

the sea floor, the intense heat from the mantle plumes generates lava that floods out to build enormous submarine volcanoes.

Sometimes these outpourings are so vast that they grow thousands of miles wide and rise above sea level. With time, most submarine volcanoes that grow tall enough for their peaks to emerge as islands eventually erode, forming submerged seamounts in the ocean again.

Submarine volcanism is widespread. Although it might be counterintuitive to imagine fire beneath the sea, it might be even harder to imagine it beneath polar ice! However, hydrothermal vents are found in all seven oceans of the world: North Pacific, South Pacific, North Atlantic, South Atlantic, Indian, Antarctic (or Southern), and Arctic Oceans[42] (Figures 1.1 and 1.3), and numerous hotspots exist over the planet.

Many volcanoes were emerging above the surface of the oceans

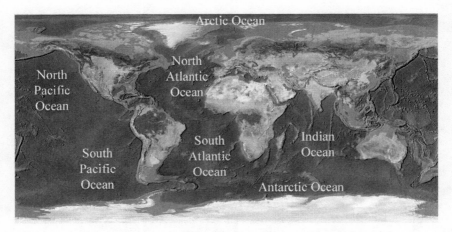

Fig 1.3. All the seven oceans of the world have submarine volcanoes.

354–206 million years ago. They created havoc and violent destruction to the environment. But that's not all.

During those times, volcanic eruptions occurred on the land, too. About 250 million years ago, eruptions occurred across thousands of miles of the Siberian continent. (Figure 2.2, p. 77) At various eras they also erupted across vast stretches of western and eastern India and under the southern Indian Ocean.

Approximately 118 million years ago, an area called the Rajmahal-Bengal-Sylhet Igneous Province on the northeastern coast of India formed from extensive volcanism associated with the nearby Kerguelen hotspot.[43] Shortly thereafter, about 112 million years ago, deep within the southern Indian Ocean, colossal volcanic outpourings began. They were caused by the distal end of the same hotspot.[44] The outpourings were amongst the largest in Earth's history. They created an enormous volcanic edifice about a third the size of the United States.[45] (Figure 1.4)

A large portion of this structure, called the Kerguelen Plateau, towered a mile above sea level.[46] Its first appearance above the ocean was about 100 million years ago. Over time, it submerged and

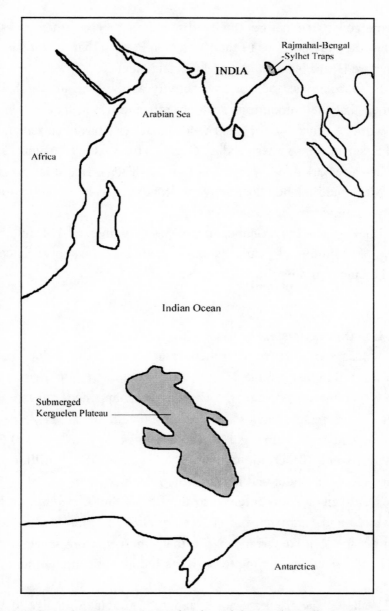

Fig 1.4. Greyed areas represent volcanic activity on the Indian subcontinent and in the southern Indian Ocean. Both are related to the Kerguelen hotspot. The activity in the ocean began shortly after that in north-east India when both areas were in close proximity 118-112 million years ago. The slow but continual movement of the Earth's tectonic plates have since increased the distance between the two areas.

re-emerged twice before finally disappearing below the waves.[47] Today, the only portions of the Kerguelen Plateau that remain above water are Heard Island and the McDonald Islands.

So furious was the volcanic activity as the plateau was being formed that the outpourings severely affected life in that region of the world.[48] Since then, violent volcanic activity has occurred again and again in the southern Indian Ocean. This vast area of land and sea has a remarkable history of volcanism. Today, Heard Island and the McDonald Islands host active volcanoes, and hydrothermal activity continues in the Indian Ocean.[49]

Luckily, the Indian subcontinent hasn't witnessed volcanic activity for millions of years. Its early igneous past has been uncovered by modern scientific discoveries.

SO SAY SCIENTISTS.

Can they be mistaken?

Let us see what Yogis millennia ago said about India's past. I'm not talking of remote history, say 5,000 or 10,000 years ago. I'm speaking of *pre*-history. Events that happened millions of years before people, says science, even existed.

Ancient texts from the 17th century to as far back as 2000 BC contain twenty descriptions that tell of a time, many millions of years ago when India was ablaze with volcanic fire.

The ancient Yogis referred to the fire as the *Aurvanala* or *Vadavanala* and *Vadavamukha*. There are also other terms. All these terms refer to a subterranean fire that emerged from beneath the land and ocean threatening to burn the Indian subcontinent and the world.

'Vadava' means mare-horse and refers metaphorically to the submarine fire's body or 'face.' The word 'Aurva' is also interesting. It's usually translated as referring to an ancient sage of that name. The sage had been born from the thigh, *uru*, of his mother and was thus named Aurva or "of the thigh." But significantly, the

58

word can also be derived from the word *urvi* which means "earth." The word Aurva, therefore, also means "of the earth" or "relating to the earth." Since the word *anala* means fire, *aurvanala* translates as the "fire of Aurva" or "fire of the earth."

As I mentioned earlier, some skeptics have difficulty understanding metaphors. Initially, such metaphors led many to believe the ancients didn't understand the subjects they spoke about. It turns out, however, that it was not the ancients who didn't know what they were talking about, but we who didn't know what *they* were talking about. It was only after many years of study that the meaning of the above metaphors became vividly clear and led to their publication in prominent science journals.

Here is a summary of the imagery depicted in the ancient texts: Hosts of divinities were concerned that India's terrestrial regions would be obliterated by the emerging subterranean fire. They therefore approached the primary heavenly being Brahma to intervene.[50] Compassionately, he had the volcanic fire consigned to the depths of the ocean south of India and all the seven oceans of the world. He instructed the fire to remain there till the next period of dissolution hundreds of millions of years in the future. The prehistoric fire arose violently above the ocean south of India at least once, and subsequently submerged. The great fire can no longer be seen in India or above its southern ocean, but it continues to exist beneath all the world's oceans. There, instead of consuming the earth, it consumes the water. Simultaneously, it rids it of its saltiness, and releases the water back into the ocean.

This is the 'mythology' recorded in the ancient literature.[51]

There are many additional details. Together, they all produce a clear image of a vast submarine volcano with a hydrothermal vent system. All the descriptions are coherent. A single convergence with science might be discarded as a fluke, but *twenty* major convergences are impossible to ignore.

Come.

Key Points to Remember

1. Volcanic eruptions devastated parts of India millions of years ago.
2. Volcanic eruptions occur in all seven oceans of the world.
3. Volcanoes have emerged above the southern Indian Ocean.
4. Volcanic fire scorched India about 118 million years ago.
5. It emerged within the southern Indian Ocean soon after – about 112 million years ago and emerged above the ocean about 100 million years ago, submerging shortly after.
6. Its emergence was cataclysmic and severely affected life forms in the area.
7. It erupted lava.
8. It had a fire pool at its center.
9. It later disappeared into the ocean.
10. The submerged structure was enormous in size.
11. Its vent areas were shiny and glittery, possibly sprinkled with gold or golden-looking particles.
12. The volcanic fire is inextinguishable, though submerged in the ocean.
13. Around the world, it continues to erupt lava at the bottom of the ocean.
14. It sucks in seawater.

15. Its mouths are the size of cracks and pores.

16. It drinks the seawater slowly.

17. It drinks it perpetually.

18. It removes salt from the water.

19. It releases the desalinated water back into the ocean.

20. It does this through another opening called a vent.

WHAT THE ANCIENT YOGIS KNEW

The divinities said:
"Lord [Brahma], a person of great splendour has been born.
In the form of fire, he has scorched
the entire surface of the earth.
O divine one, if the surface of the earth is destroyed ...
that inevitably leads to our annihilation."

Then Brahma went to Aurva and said to him:
"Why are you burning the earth?
Desist at once for my sake, o supreme priest."

Aurva said:
I myself am stopping now at your request, o truest one.
[But] some stratagem must be construed
so that this fire
that I have released should go into the ocean.

Then Brahma, invoking his divine daughter, said:
"Daughter, grab the fire and go to the sea.
Go quickly, o brilliant lady."

Skanda Purana (Prabhasa Khanda) 7.35.9-17

When you first cried as you were born,
rising from the ocean or from the land ...
that is your celebrated birth, o horse.

VOLCANOES UNDER THE SEA

You are the back of water,
the womb of fire,
growing to might,
the ocean swelling all around.

Yajur Veda, Taittiriya Samhita 4.2.8.1

The fire arose from the ocean or the land.
It roared ('cried') at birth.
It grew in might.

Thereupon that horse-bodied,
bright [fire] lit by a garland of flame
entered the ocean,
readily burning up the floods of its water.

Shiva Purana (Rudra Samhita).3 (Parvati Khanda).20.21

Aurva released that fire ... into the ocean,
and it consumes water in the ocean.
It drinks water in the ocean,
vomiting that fire from its mouth.

Mahabharata 1.171.21-22

As well as drinking the ocean's water, the fire spews lava
at the bottom of the ocean.

I invoke the pure fire,
dwelling in the midst of the sea.

Rig Veda Samhita 8:102.4, 2.7.3-4, 2.35.3, and Yajur Veda, Taittiriya Samhita, 3.1.11

(This reference to the fire dwelling in the ocean is the oldest
– at least 1500 BC.)

And the great fire settles down in the ocean,
drinking water little by little.

Brahma Purana 110.210

The blazing fire of Aurva
drinks up the water of the seven seas.

Yoga Vasishta 6.2.66.24

The horse-fire drinks the waters ...
and releases those same [waters].

Brahma Purana 56.21cd-22ab

In a golden [or shiny] vessel ...
is the horse-fire, pin-mouthed and large-bodied.
It drinks water forever.
In this era (*manvantara*) it has become invisible in the sea,
declaredly in the southern direction.

Skanda Purana (Prabhasa Khanda).29.92-97ab

The submerged structure appears golden or shiny.
It is submerged in the Indian ocean towards the south.

He [Aurva] made his mouth equal to the eye of a needle.
His mouth drank water
in a way like the working of a waterclock.

Skanda Purana (Prabhasa Khanda) 7.33.99-101

The submerged structure sucks in water slowly.

The Vadavanala Fire exists in the ocean
but because of its tremendous size
is not extinguished by the ocean.

Vachanamruta, Gadhada, I.72

Where ... the seven great seas
with gems and jewels as their lotus roots,
and with the fire of Aurva
for their lotus flowers ... .

Yoga Vasishta 4.53.13

The Aurva fire exists in the seven oceans of the world.
Beds of the seven seas are strewn with precious looking gems and jewels.

In the sea, there is that great fire.
Its gruel is said to be that swiftly rippling water
along with the animate and inanimate beings in it.

And there the roar of
helpless water-dwelling creatures can be heard,
crying out when they glimpse

that horse-face fire.

Ramayana 4.39.42-44

This [salty] water of the ocean shall become sweet
as it is drunk by that [fire] named Vadavamukha.
This water of the ocean is even now being drunk
by that [fire] named Vadavamukha.

Mahabharata 12.329.48

The Vadavanala Fire exists in the ocean
but is not extinguished by it.
It drinks the seawater
and removes its saltiness.
It then expels the water from another opening.

Vachanamruta, Vartal 3

Modern science has discovered the prehistoric conflagration of
India by volcanism and all these characteristics of submarine volcanoes and their hydrothermal vents only recently.

But ancient Yogis were able to describe them millennia ago.

They said there is volcanic fire in all the seven oceans of the world; they spoke of its emergence in India and in the ocean south of India millions of years ago; the volcanic structure was huge and had risen above sea-level and later submerged; the fiery structure continues to 'vomit' lava at the bottom of the ocean; because the source of its fire is so enormous, the water cannot extinguish it; the submerged structure appears golden and strewn with glittery gems; the structure continues to draw in water from mouths the size of needle holes, or minute pores and it ejects this water from another opening. Lastly, the fire removes salt from the water.

How can all these descriptions be by accident?

Let us inspect another important description: the timeframe. Is there agreement with science here, too?

Science estimates India was beset by volcanic activity due to the Kerguelen hotspot about 118 million years ago. That same fire then appeared within the ocean south of India about 112 million years ago, and then above its surface about 100 million years ago. It submerged a little later. Everything happened between around 118 million to 100 million years ago.

What timeframe did the Yogis give? 6,000 years ago? 6 trillion years ago? No.

Between 120.9-117.5 million years ago. (Workshop 1)

A splendid convergence with scientific estimates.

How could ancient Yogis millennia ago give twenty accurate details of a volcanic phenomenon that occurs well outside of our normal experience 1.4 miles beneath the oceans, and which occurred around 100 million years ago in India and in the southern Indian Ocean?

How did they arrive at these correct conclusions?

By chance, hope beleaguered skeptics. Surely, they plead, these extensive convergences are the 'only' valid ones of modern science and ancient spirituality. Indeed, upon witnessing so many, some skeptics, like the scientist who denied there's a correspondence between ancient literature and salt-depleting hydrothermal vents, might bury their heads even deeper in the sand. Sadly, they've decided one way, and there may be no changing them. It seems their minds are clenched shut even against objective studies and numerous correspondences like these.

Even sadder, some skeptics think they're smarter than the rest of the world, including scientists with superior credentials who disagree with them on this matter! Their ignorance and arrogance has almost reached the point of being humorous. The disservice they do to spirituality, however, is far from funny. They are attacking the very soul of humanity, the spirit of human civilization.

Thankfully, these undeniable convergences have emerged and they forcefully rebut the naysayer's myopic, physical view of the world. Their thick books attacking spirituality and God's existence can now be tossed onto the growing scrapheap of discredited pseudoscientific ideas.

Ironically, though, in some ways their myopic view of the universe is actually correct. Truly speaking, the physical cosmos is a comparatively tiny body floating in the unfathomable, infinite, and transcendental mind of God. It's all about context.

Back to the convergences.

As I researched the correspondences between submarine volcanoes and the Vadavanala Agni of the Yogis, several passages led me to consider something else.

Did this volcanic fire also emerge at an earlier era than this? If so, how did it affect the planet and life? Might it be connected to the worldwide extinction and Flood described in the Bible?

Workshop 1

In the first Treta age of this era (manvantara),
[the fire] is hidden in the sea in the southern direction.
(Skanda Purana, Prabhasa Khanda 7.1.29:93-94 & 7.1.34:34-37)

Clearly, the volcanic fire disappeared into the sea south of India sometime during the first Treta age of this manvantara. By implication, it means the fire must have scorched India shortly before this era during the Satya Yuga or more probably during the last Kali Yuga ('dark age') of the previous manvantara.

What do these terms the 'Treta,' 'Satya' and 'Kali' of a 'manvantara' era refer to?

The ancient Yogis spoke of immense time scales when they spoke of the history of our Earth and universe. They divided it into various eons, eras, epochs, and ages. These were kalpas, manvantaras, maha yugas, and yugas. A kalpa is immensely long. It lasts 4.32 *billion* years and consists of 14 manvantaras along with some brief and negligible transition periods. Each of these manvantaras consists of 71 epochs known as maha yugas or 'chatur yugas.'[52] Each manvantara is therefore about 308.5 million years in length. Each of the chatur yugas is 4.32 million years long.[53] A thousand of them exactly equals a kalpa. Furthermore, each chatur yuga comprises 4 ages called Satya, Treta, Dvapara, and Kali. Satya lasts 1,728,000 years; Treta lasts 1,296,000 years; Dvapara lasts 864,000 years; and Kali lasts 432,000 years. We're presently in the beginning of the Kali Yuga of the 28th Maha Yuga of the 7th Manvantara, called the Vaivasvata Manvantara. (*Markandeya Purana* 50.7) It's traditionally believed that Kali began about 5,000 years ago.

This means the *first* Treta age of this manvantara that saw the submergence of the volcanic fire in the Indian Ocean began (counting backwards):

Part Kali + 1 Dvapara + 1 Treta + 1 Satya + 26 Maha Yugas
+ 1 Kali + 1 Dvapara + 1 Treta
= 5,000 + 864,000 + 1,296,000 + 1,728,000 + (26 x 4.32 million) + 432,000
+ 864,000 + 1,296,000

= 118,805,000 years ago

and ended:

Part Kali + 1 Dvapara + 1 Treta + 1 Satya + 26 Maha Yugas
+ 1 Kali + 1 Dvapara
= 5,000 + 864,000 + 1,296,000 + 1,728,000 + (26 x 4.32 million)

$$+ 432,000 + 864,000$$

$$= 117,509,000 \text{ years ago}$$

This is roughly between 118.8-117.5 million years ago.

***

The era before the first Treta age of this manvantara, that is the Satya Yuga, or more probably the last Kali Yuga of the previous manvantara, that saw the emergence of the volcanic fire in India began (counting backwards):

Part Kali + 1 Dvapara + 1 Treta + 1 Satya + 26 Maha Yugas
+ 1 Kali + 1 Dvapara + 1 Treta + 1 Satya + 1 Kali
$$= 5,000 + 864,000 + 1,296,000 + 1,728,000 + (26 \times 4.32 \text{ million}) + 432,000$$
$$+ 864,000 + 1,296,000 + 1,728,000 + 432,000$$

$$= 120,965,000 \text{ years ago}$$

The entire episode from scorching of India by volcanic fire to the submergence of this fire in the Indian Ocean occurred between

$$= 120,965,000 \text{ to } 117,509,000 \text{ years ago}$$

This is roughly between 120.9-117.5 million years ago

ANCIENT GLOBAL EXTINCTION

TODAY IS A RELATIVELY DRY AND TEMPERATE world compared to earlier eons. About four billion years ago, our planet was probably a waterworld almost entirely engulfed by a single ocean.[54]

The life and history of our planet is remarkable. During its earliest times, the Earth wasn't anything like you see today. Those were days of climatic turmoil and instability. Luckily, they were also punctuated with periods of great development. Even the most dire circumstances didn't destroy our planet.

Earth is a survivor.

Its epic legacy began 4.5 billion years ago when it was born. A molten ball of rock, the embryonic Earth had no atmosphere or oceans. Meteors and asteroids smashed into it ceaselessly. But it absorbed the punches and they turned to its advantage. The stuff hurtling at it from outer space carried something precious. Water. Lots of it.

Shallow pools swelled into great oceans and, until 2.8-2.5 billion years ago, bathed much of the planet.[55] Except for primitive organisms that appeared between 3 and 4 billion years ago, it was quite lifeless. There were no fish, animals, birds, or plants. The only creatures that existed were bacteria. Beneath the ocean, however, the planet was stirring. The continents were beginning to form.

One by one, all over the Earth, pieces of land clamored above the ocean surface between 2.5-2 billion years ago.[56] The continents were born. By this time, most of today's landmass had emerged above the sea. But they were not in today's configurations. They looked different. A process called plate tectonics shifted them over the Earth like pieces of a jigsaw. Sometimes they came together and sometimes apart. Each interaction led to modified shapes and configurations. The slow process continues even today.

Shortly after the initial period of momentous upheaval, about 1.8 billion years ago, simple plants, fungi, and animals arose.

It was a small family.

But not for long. A rowdy and colorful crowd appeared between 545-490 million years ago. This marvelous episode is famously known as the 'Cambrian Explosion.'

Then, between 417-354 million years ago, during the Devonian era or the 'era of fish,' numerous types appeared – many of them armored and jawed. Predatory, some grew to monstrous sizes of 20-30 feet in length. Shark-like, they were formidable predators.[57] Other fish such as the *Xenacanthus* were much smaller – just 2-3 feet in length. It had a defensive spine like a horn on its head. (Figure 2.1[58])

Life in the water was vicious and dangerous.

It was literally a fish-eat-fish world.[59]

Another interesting period ensued between 290-248 million years ago. It's called the Permian era. During this period, due to plate tectonics, continents of the world came together. Approaching each other for millions of years, they finally collided and fused into a single landmass. This supercontinent was surrounded by a single sea, a superocean. (Figure 2.2)

Imagine a stretch of land larger than the United States, Canada,

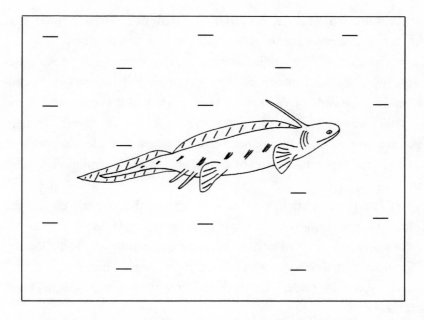

Fig 2.1. The 2 feet long *Xenacanthus* had a defensive spine or 'horn' on its head. (Artist's impression.)

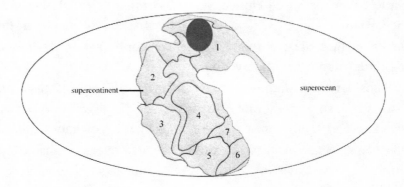

Fig 2.2. Shadowed area indicates the region of Siberian volcanism on the supercontinent. A close look at the shapes within the 'jigsaw' reveal the continents we are familiar with today. 1. Eurasia 2. North America 3. South America 4. Africa 5. Antarctica 6. Australia 7. India.

South America, Russia, and Africa combined. Now add to that Australia, Europe, China, India and the rest of the world. It was a carpet of land so vast, its inner regions, distant from the ocean, became hot, dry, and scorched. Most probably there was little rain there for hundreds of years.[60] Instead, perpetual drought reigned.

But more devastating events followed. As though things weren't bad enough, the planet suffered an enormous outpouring of lava on the Siberian continent at the end of the Permian era. (Figure 2.2)

It led to an extinction far worse than that which ended the reign of large dinosaurs. Known as 'The Great Dying,' it occurred across the end of the Permian era and beginning of the following Triassic era. It was so severe, life on Earth nearly ended.

By some estimates, ninety-five percent of living species were wiped out.[61]

How did this happen?

There doesn't seem to be one single cause, but several contemporaneous and connected ones. Scientists are still debating them today. However, this much is known for sure. The Siberian continent erupted with such volcanic intensity, it effused enough lava to cover the entire United States 2-3 miles thick. Rather than tall volcanoes, the lava issued from long fissures or cracks in the Earth's surface. The extreme volcanism continued for a hellish long time – about a million years!

Consider the voluminous toxic material – lava, ash, dust, and poisonous gases – the eruptions must have disgorged into the atmosphere and their impact on life. In general, volcanoes release hydrogen sulfide and sulfur dioxide. They also release chlorine and fluorine.[62] These destroy our Earth's ozone layer. It's a crucial shield around our planet that prevents harmful ultraviolet light from the Sun reaching the planet's surface. The destruction to the ozone layer was calamitous. Small life forms such as insects are extremely resistant to extinction. But ultraviolet rays kill them rapidly. Indeed, one of the hallmarks of the Permian-Triassic extinction is that it wiped out even small life forms.[63]

Another perilous emission of volcanoes is carbon dioxide. Recently, this has become well known due to its role in global warming. This would have caused our planet to heat up significantly and intensify environmental stress.

Out of all the gases released by volcanoes, however, water vapor is the most abundant. Consider this. While simply sitting dormant, a volcano can emit between 10 million to 1,000 million tons of gas per year. But it could release the same amount during a single eruption lasting just a few hours or days.[64] Now imagine the equivalent of hundreds of volcanoes erupting across *a million* years.[65] This is what occurred in Siberia towards the end of the Permian era 251 million years ago!

Toxic gases poisoned the atmosphere globally. Chlorine and fluorine depleted the ozone layer. This allowed the Sun's ultraviolet rays to fry the planet's surface and kill off small life forms. Steam from the volcanoes created great clouds and saturated the air. The skies were filled with lightning, ash, and dust. The atmosphere became heated due to the fire of the volcanism as well as the greenhouse effect of carbon dioxide and water vapor. The oceans also became heated and less able to retain oxygen. This promoted the growth of anaerobic bacteria. In turn, they released deadly hydrogen sulphide and began the extinction of life in the oceans. Its release into the atmosphere would also have hurt the ozone layer allowing even more ultraviolet light to fry the planet.[66] Eventually, volcanic dust in the atmosphere blocked the Sun and the atmosphere cooled. Torrential acid rain poured and deluged the land. Sea levels rose across the Permian-Triassic boundary[67] and between 240-200 million years ago, there was flooding of many continents worldwide. Significant parts of North America, western South America, the British Isles, Arctic Norway, Europe, Africa, and the Middle East were underwater.[68] Called 'epeiric' seas, these temporary oceans retreated and returned to various degrees over various countries and periods. Depending on the elevation of the ground, the water was from fifty to several hundred meters deep.[69]

There would have been a *flood* of fire – as lava flowed for a million years, accompanied by torrential rains and inward migrating seas. Life, small and large, on land and in the oceans, was almost wiped out.

The Permian-Triassic extinction was like none other in the history of our planet. There were extinctions before and after it, the most famous of these being the extinction of large dinosaurs about 66 million years ago. But these extinctions were 'minor' in comparison. Extinctions such as that of most dinosaurs may serve as dramatic material for movies, but from a historical perspective, none of these extinction episodes compare to the grassroots level of extinction that occurred during the Permian-Triassic.

The difference is that after other extinctions, life seems to have picked up very close to where it left off, albeit evolving in new directions. But the Permian-Triassic extinction was *quite* different. The life forms appearing after it seem so distinct from the previous ones, some nineteenth century scientists thought they were from a completely new creation event.[70]

Scientists therefore view the Permian-Triassic extinction as a pivotal turning point in the history of life on our planet. It cleared the stage on the continents and in the oceans for the appearance of a new cast of characters. Its repercussions are unmatched by any of the extinctions that happened before it, or ever since.

Fortunately, during the Permian-Triassic, not all life was annihilated. Some species survived.

But there was more volcanism about 50 million years later.[71] During this period known as the end-Triassic, the eruptions were comparable to those in Siberia. Much of the lava was erupting explosively above the Atlantic Ocean from mid-ocean ridges in an area called the Central Atlantic Magmatic Province (CAMP).[72] All this led to yet another extinction. It occurred across the end-Triassic and beginning of the following Jurassic. What is truly astounding about this extinction is that it seems to have wiped out many of the few survivors of the Permian-Triassic! It's as though nature was determined to leave no trace of any pre-Permian life forms.

The emergence of these enormous volcanic ridges dealt a double whammy to the Earth and its inhabitants. Not only did this volcanism poison the atmosphere, it also displaced a colossal volume of water that deluged the continents. After receding for about 25 million years, ocean levels rose again[73] and between 175-112 million years ago, much of the continents were again flooded. Many places across the world, including western North America, eastern Greenland, eastern Africa, and Europe, were submerged.[74] Kutch in northwest India was also submerged. Back then, of course, these continents were not in their present day positions.

Sea-levels and flooding continued to increase till about 70 million years ago and thereafter receded rapidly towards current levels. After the extinction of large dinosaurs about 66 million years ago, here we are today, surrounded by a bounty of life forms belonging to numerous species.[75]

In biology, the term 'species' refers to classes of similar creatures that can potentially interbreed and produce fertile offspring. How many such species are there today, exactly? This has been a difficult question for scientists to answer right up until 2011. Previous estimates were so speculative they ranged between 3-100 million species.[76] Now, better methods have chafed it down more accurately to about 8.7 million species.[77]

Here is a timeline of when various life forms appeared on Earth: As we saw, about 4 billion years ago, our planet was probably submerged in a global ocean.[78] The earliest living organisms were single-celled anaerobic microbes called archeans and appeared in the oceans roughly 3.5 billion years ago, probably feeding off fluids from hydrothermal vents.[79] Various types of bacteria also appeared and flourished. Some bacteria used the Sun's energy for photosynthesis and released oxygen into the atmosphere. Oxygen concentrations reached a critical level roughly 2.4 billion years ago that killed off many anaerobic species.[80] Green algae appeared about 1.4 billion years ago and multi-celled organisms about 1 billion years ago. Visible soft-bodied multicellular life forms such as sponges appeared about 630 million years ago. Large animal life such as mollusks and arthropods with hard protective shells and exoskeletons appeared 543 million years ago.[81] Swimming animals such as some trilobites appeared about 500 million years ago. The first fish – which were jawless – appeared about 530 million years ago.[82] Large, armored, and jawed fish that preyed on other fish appeared between 417-354 million years ago. There is evidence that animal life moved onto land about 370 million years ago.[83] Dinosaurs appeared about 240 million years ago (and all but birds went extinct 65 million years ago). About 150 million years ago, early birds took to the skies.[84] Only after 60 million years ago did hunting, carnivorous cats and dogs appear. Early horses and elephants also appeared.[85] Then, 2.5-2 million years ago, early relatives of humans arrived, like the tool-making *Homo habilis*, the 'handy man.'[86] And here we all are today.

Here, then, was a simplified account of complex and overlapping events that occurred across four billion years of Earth's history. All this is impossible to know without the tools of modern science.

AGAIN, SO SAY SCIENTISTS.

Are they right? Or could ancient Yogis have known this, too, as they clearly did concerning submarine volcanoes and hydrothermal vents in India's prehistoric past? Is it possible those Yogis could peer into even more remote periods such as the fish-eat-fish Devonian era and the Permian-Triassic era, too?

ANCIENT GLOBAL EXTINCTION

Indeed, like the Sages of the Bible, the Yogis spoke of a period on Earth millions of years ago when nearly all life was wiped out. They said it was related to intense volcanic activity and global flooding. The following imagery is found in the Yoga Literature. Some of it dates back to at least 1000 BC.

Millions of years ago, a celestial patriarch of the Earth was ruler over the welfare of the world. This heavenly being was its wise, virtuous, and seventh patriarch. His name was Vaivasvata Manu. God appeared to Manu in the form of a fish in a river. Initially, the Fish Avatar was small, but grew so large, Manu needed to relocate it in the ocean. The fish had a horn or spine on its head. It described to Manu impending volcanic activity and global flooding. These would lead to extinction of life worldwide. Manu was to place the seeds of all life-forms in an Ark for protection and use them to restore life on Earth after the extinction.

Their conversation was as follows.

Key Points to Remember

1. The Earth was once a vicious 'fish-eat-fish' world (Devonian era).
2. This was between 417-354 million years ago.
3. After this, life on Earth faced near total extinction.
4. This occurred around 251 million years ago (Permian-Triassic era).
5. The extinction began with the land becoming scorched and dry.
6. The Sun's rays were overbearing and killed off small organisms.
7. Volcanoes emerged from the land and oceans.
8. They erupted violently and ejected fire that burnt the land and heated the skies.
9. They ejected poisonous gases.
10. They ejected steam.
11. The steam and gases formed into clouds of destruction.
12. Lightning filled the skies.
13. The clouds rained torrentially and inundated the land.
14. Ocean levels were rising. Between 240-200 million years ago, many continents were flooded by seas.
15. Volcanoes arose from the mid-Atlantic Ocean and around 200 million years ago (end-Triassic era) there was a 'followup' extinction that killed off many survivors of the Permian-Triassic.

16. Ocean levels continued to rise and flooded large parts of many continents worldwide.
17. This occurred between 175-112 million years ago.
18. Associated with all the above events, there was worldwide extinction of life.
19. Some life forms survived and repopulated the Earth.
20. Today, there are about 8.7 million species.

WHAT THE ANCIENT YOGIS KNEW

The Fish Avatar said:
"There is much danger for us [fish] so long as we are small
— fish verily devour fish.

Shatapatha Brahmana 1.8.1.3

The pre-extinction period was a vicious fish-eat-fish world.

The Fish Avatar said:
I am a small fish. I am afraid of strong fish,
therefore please save me.
For strong fish devour weak fish in particular.

Mahabharata 3.185.7-8

The Fish Avatar said:
"Don't throw me back into the river, most excellent of men.
I'm afraid of sharks and such [large predators] there."

Agni Purana 2.5-6

The Fish Avatar said:
In a short time, the earth
shall be drowned in water
along with its mountains, wildernesses, and forests.

This ship has been built
by the congregation of all divinities
for the purpose of saving
the great congregation of living beings, o king.

O man faithful to your vows,
put them all in this ship
and protect them who have no protector:
[all] those born of putrefaction and those born of eggs,
those that sprout, as well as those beings born of womb.

When, o king, the ship is lashed
by the gales of the end of the age,
you shall then tie it to this horn of mine.

Matsya Purana 1.29-32

The king asked:
"O bounteous Lord, in how many years
will the destruction of the era happen?
And how, o my Lord, shall I protect the beings?

And how shall I meet you again?"

Matsya Purana 2.1-2cd

The Fish Avatar said:
"Beginning with today,
there will be a drought on the earth
for a full hundred years,
a famine that brings devastation.

Then the Sun shall have terrible rays
that shower [like] burning coals
and bring a destruction of lesser beings.

At the end of the age,
the Aurva fire [in the ocean] will also be agitated,
and so also the poison-fire from the underworld ... .

Matsya Purana 3-5

The land shall be dried and scorched.
The Sun's rays will kill off small organisms.
Volcanic fire shall emerge from the ocean and land.

The Fish Avatar said:

When the whole earth,
having been thus burnt up, becomes like ash,
the sky shall heat up with steam.

The seven clouds of destruction,
arising from the copious steam generated by the fire
shall inundate the earth.

And the oceans, becoming turbulent, shall be united
and turn this entire world into a single ocean.

[Then] taking hold of this ship ...
putting aboard all sorts of creature-seeds,
and tying the ship to my horn
using the rope given by me,
o man faithful to your vows, protected by me,
you alone shall remain.

Matsya Purana 2.1-2ab, 6-12

The Fish Avatar said:
Thou shall build a strong massive ark
and have it furnished with a long rope.
On that [ark] must thou ascend ...
and take with thee all the different seeds ...
and separately and carefully
must thou preserve them therein.[87]

GOD IS REAL

Mahabharata 3.186.29-30

When the time described by the Lord arrived as foretold,
he appeared in the form of a horned fish.

Matsya Purana 2.17

In that year which [the fish Avatar] designated,
[the king] fashioned a ship and approached [the Avatar].

When the flood rose, he entered the ship.
That fish swam down next to him.
[The king] fastened the ship's rope to its horn.
By means of that, [the king] moved swiftly to
this northern mountain ... .

The fish Avatar said: "I have saved you.
Tie the ship to a tree, lest the water cut you off
[from the ship] while you are on the mountain.

As the water gradually descends,
you shall follow it down always that much."
He followed it down always that much.

And thus this [side?] of the northern mountain

ANCIENT GLOBAL EXTINCTION

is [called] "the descent of Manu."

The flood had indeed
carried away all those [other] creatures.

Shatapatha Brahmana 1.8.1.4-7

[Today] by four modes of birth[88]
are produced 8.4 million species
(or classes) [of creatures],
inhabiting the air, the water, and the earth.

Ramacharitamanasa, Bala Kanda 1.7.1[89]

8.4 million species (or classes)
were originally created:
those born from sprouts,
those born from putrefaction,
those born from eggs and those born from wombs.

Garuda Purana 2.3.42, 104cd-105ab; Devi Bhagata Purana 3.7.52

There are 8.4 million species
of creatures.

Vachanamruta, Gadhada I.21, 37, 44; Kariyani 7; Gadhada III.14, 19; Bhugol Khagol

Is this ancient account a depiction of the fish-eat-fish Devonian era, followed by the Permian-Triassic extinction, extensive flooding worldwide, the 'follow-up' end-Triassic extinction, and subsequent extensive flooding again between 417-112 million years ago?

The biological, geological, and climatological events match closely. First there was the fish-eat-fish era. Then the land became heated and parched. The piercing rays of the Sun were as hot as coal and destroyed small creatures. Volcanoes emerged from beneath the land and sea. They spewed fire and ejected steam, poisonous fumes, and ash into the atmosphere. The skies were heated. The ground turned to ash. The volcanic gases created destructive clouds. These led to torrential rains that inundated the land. Agitated seas breached their shores and rose to heights that flooded the continents. Plants and animals worldwide, during all this, were wiped out. Some survived and today there are 8.4 million species.

These convergences with science are extensive, but how can it be possible? Surely nobody can know the Earth's ancient past without the tools of modern science? All this happened between 417-112 million years ago, stretching across four eras. Moreover, how could the Yogis know the correct number of species in existence today?

Ancient Yogis meditating under a tree couldn't know all this about the present or past, surely? Indeed, if they gave a date for the extinction, for example, wouldn't it be too recent, something like 10,000 years ago? Or something too far back, like 10 trillion years ago?

Astoundingly, no.

They *did* give a date, in fact. They said it all occurred between 429-120.5 million years ago.

Another major convergence with science! (Workshop 2) The question arises, How did the Yogis even know there was a global extinction, let alone know its timeframe? There is no known way other than the spiritual way.

BEFORE WE PROCEED FURTHER, you will have observed that the story of Vaivasvata Manu has unmistakable convergences with that of Noah and the Great Flood described in the Bible. This flood inundated the Earth globally and wiped out nearly all life.

[God:] I, do bring the flood of waters on this earth,
to destroy all flesh having the breath of life from under the sky.
Everything that is in the earth will die.

Bible, Genesis 6:17

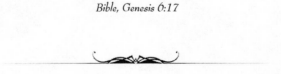

The only surviver of the flood was a virtuous individual named Noah, his family, and various life forms he was entrusted to preserve in order to repopulate the Earth. For this purpose, he was instructed by God to build an Ark that would protect them during the flood and torrential rains. During the aftermath, his ship was led to a mountaintop where all its occupants disembarked. This is the core of the Biblical legend and there is little doubt that the Bible and Yoga Literature refer to one and the same life-annihilating global crisis.

Genuine spiritual revelation is similar everywhere. (Section 5)

The Bible is true. That the Yogis and Israelites possessed all this knowledge is astounding. But did our planet comprise the limit of their knowledge?

The convergences I saw between modern science and the ancient Vadavanala's involvement in this global extinction, its later scorching of India, and emergence above the Indian Ocean emboldened me to pursue the trail further.

Did the ancient Yogis and Israelites know things beyond our Earth?

Workshop 2

[Everything] thus becomes a single ocean (*ekarnava*) at the end
of Chakshusha's manvantara era."
Matsya Purana 2.14

This ancient passage states that the volcanic activity, flooding and extinction of life worldwide occurred during and till the end of the Chakshusha Manvantara. When did this Manvantara begin and end?

You saw in the last section how the ancient Yogis divided the history of our planet and indeed the universe into various eons, eras, epochs, and ages. These were kalpas, manvantaras, maha yugas, and yugas. A kalpa is immensely long. It lasts 4.32 *billion* years and consists of 14 manvantaras. Each of these consists of 71 epochs known as 'chatur yugas' or maha yugas. Each manvantara is therefore about 308.5 million years in length. The current manvantara, known as the Vaivasvata Manvantara, proceeded directly after the Chakshusha Manvantara. The Vaivasvata is the seventh manvantara and has passed through 27 of its 71 maha yugas. It is currently at the beginning of the Kali Yuga of the 28th maha yuga. This means the Chakshusha Manvantara began the following number of years ago (counting backwards):

Part Kali + 1 Dvapara + 1 Treta + 1 Satya + 27 Maha Yugas of Vaivasvata
+ 71 Maha Yugas of Chakshusha
= 5,000 + 864,000 + 1,296,000 + 1,728,000 + (27 x 4.32 million)
+ (71 x 4.32 million)

= 429,033,000 years ago

and ended:

Part Kali + 1 Dvapara + 1 Treta + 1 Satya + 27 Maha Yugas of Vaivasvata
= 5,000 + 864,000 + 1,296,000 + 1,728,000 + (27 x 4.32 million)

= 120,533,000 years ago

This is roughly between about 429-120.5 million years ago.

Section

THE BIG BANG AND OUR GALAXY

ANYONE WHO HAS LIVED AWAY from a big city and peered into the night sky will have seen a sight they could never forget. A myriad of sparkling stars shining in the thousands like pearls and diamonds scattered upon a canopy of black velvet. This is nature's jewel shop, cosmic in size, astronomical in age. (Figure 3.1)

Unfortunately, the stunning heavens are obscured by city lights and many people rarely have time to pause and wonder. But in ancient times, the sky was visible to all, and people marveled at what they saw. What were these 'lights'? How far away were they? Where did they come from?

The answers took millennia to arrive. When they did, the world would never be the same.

After Galileo pointed his telescope at the sky in 1602, astronomers in the 1700s noticed hundreds of fuzzy patches of light nestled amongst the stars. They called them 'nebulae.' Astronomers wondered what they were. Thus began the great debate: What were these structures and how far were they? Were they just a few stars blurred by their distance? May be, but even the best of telescopes couldn't resolve them into individual stars.

Fig 3.1. ESO's Paranal Observatory in Chile. A laser guide points across the southern sky towards the center of the Milky Way. Image credit: ESO/Y. Beletsky.

In 1781, the British astronomer William Herschel built a telescope truly brilliant for its time. Training it towards the nebulae, he was amazed to see that they comprised *millions* of stars that were so far away they appeared as fuzzy patches to lesser instruments.

Later, in 1925, the American astronomer Edwin Hubble showed they were 'island universes.'

So great in size were these islands, they were universes in their own right. Our own starry system is itself an island universe – one amongst billions of others. The new paradigm is that we live on a minute but beautiful speck of dust floating amongst billions of stars comprising one island universe, drifting amongst billions of other island universes, none of which has a privileged central position in space. This is known as the Cosmological Principle. The universe has no center.

Gradually, the term island universe was replaced with the familiar term 'galaxy.' This is because they are not quite islands. Though they seem to be widely dispersed and isolated from each other, they strongly interact. They are components of a larger system.

Our own galaxy is referred to simply as the 'Galaxy' with a capital G, or as the 'Milky Way.'

Since Hubble, state-of-the-art instruments like the Hubble Space Telescope (named after him) combined with powerful mathematical theorems and supercomputers have helped scientists to fathom the nature of our universe – when it was created, how it evolved, and what it will look like in the future.

The new discoveries are enthralling.

IN THE BEGINNING ...

Prior to 13.7 billion years ago, our universe didn't exist. There were no galaxies, stars, matter, or even space.

There was *one* thing, however. Scientists don't know much about it, but they call it a 'singularity.' A singularity is not nothing. It's a tiny seed smaller than the size of an atom. For some reason, it suddenly expanded and inside it sprung the whole observable universe – space, time, gases, stars, and eventually, galaxies. That creative moment 13.7 billion years ago is commonly called the 'Big Bang.'

Its discovery is science's greatest. Sadly, the history of all the people behind it is not often told.

Why?

Before the 1920s, pretty much nobody had any idea how this universe came to be. Scientists simply assumed it had always been here. They didn't believe there was a creation moment. That was the naive belief of spiritual people. In their scientific opinion, the universe must always have existed. From eternity. It was never created.

But this was soon to change. Astronomers such as Vesto Slipher discovered in the 1900s evidence that galaxies were in motion, some floating towards and some away from us.[90] These galaxies were 'red-shifted.' Hubble also noticed the red-shifts and conducted many detailed studies.

He, however, was doubtful of their meaning. He published many papers criticizing the conclusions of others that the galaxies were receding. This included his last paper in 1953. Throughout his life, Hubble was skeptical of the expansion of the universe. He felt his data was better understood depicting *apparent* recession. The expansion was an illusion.[91]

It was in 1922 that the expansion of the universe was first proposed. The idea didn't come from Hubble or Albert Einstein. It came from a Russian. His name was Aleksandr Freidmann. The genius mathematician showed Einstein's static universe was unstable.[92] It would lead to expansion.[93]

Then, out of the blue from Belgium appeared a Christian priest. He was a talented mathematician named Georges Lemaitre. Upon studying all the evidence, and unaware of Freidmann's work, he independently concluded that the universe must be expanding. He even published a paper in 1927 announcing his discovery.[94]

But he was brushed aside – even by Einstein who said his calculations were correct, but his physics was "abominable."

In hindsight, we find it difficult to understand what drove Einstein to do this. But it does indicate how difficult it was for scientists to accept the possibility of an expanding universe or a possible 'creation event.'[95] It was a nerve-racking revelation to them.

Initially, many resisted, and the world's finest scientist, Einstein, was amongst them.

Meanwhile, many other distinguished scientists such as Arthur Eddington, who was a former teacher of Lemaitre, were struggling to interpret the findings.

What did the redshifts mean? They were baffled.

Lemaitre wrote and reminded Eddington of his expanding universe theory. This time he won him to his side. Now Eddington became a champion of Lemaitre's cause. The illustrious scientist announced that the universe must indeed be expanding, as his priest-student had concluded.

Though expensive telescopes are named after Hubble today, even a trained scientist like himself missed the discovery of the millennium. In contrast, it's perhaps prognostic that the great discovery came from a man of spirituality. Even in his youth, Lemaitre had proclaimed there was "no conflict between science and religion."[96]

Today, scientists know that during the earliest moments of creation, the first things to emerge were space and time. This is usually referred to as *spacetime*, a continuum. They seem to be closely related and intertwined. But for much of history, scientists thought that space was an absolute void, an absence, pure nothingness. Now they know this isn't true. Space is actually a substance, a material. Due to the Big Bang, this space-fabric was literally stretched out to create the vast area we call the universe.

About a second after the Big Bang, a sea of atomic particles such as protons, neutrons, and electrons evolved from an ocean of energy.[97] Out of these, gases formed. Most abundant was hydrogen. By the force of gravity, these gases gathered into a grand network of filaments branching in every direction of the universe.

Naturally, gas was denser where the filaments crossed. This gas became the building material of the first stars and and so it was at those intersections that galaxies first formed.[98] (Figure 3.2)

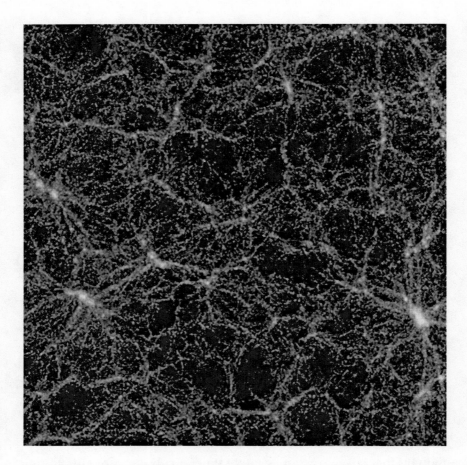

Fig 3.2. Computer-simulated image of primordial gases from the Big Bang formed into a network of filaments like a creeper-vine stretching across space. Bright points are galaxies at its nodes. Dark patches are vast voids in between. Image credit: Volker Springel, Max-Planck-Institute for Astrophysics, Garching, Germany.

OUR GALAXY IS BORN

Due to the continued effects of gravity, the hydrogen collected into balls. These condensed and ignited into spheroids of fire. Stars were born. They were the first members of our developing, disheveled Galaxy.[99] Enormous and extremely luminous, they exploded as 'supernovae' soon after birth. Billions of them continued to appear, burning brightly, many still exploding. It was an Olympic opening ceremony of galactic proportions. It was a blazing beginning, a galaxy spawning numerous stars for around three billion years.[100] A gorgeous fireworks display, each exploding star could outshine our entire Galaxy.[101]

It would have been a marvelous sight. As these new stars began to appear, they and the proto-galaxies of which they were members, collided to form the halo of our Galaxy. This gave our Galaxy the appearance of an extremely effulgent rudimentary spheroid. It would have been a shining cocoon in the barrenness of space. It was the first structure of our Galaxy to form and it still exists. Very ancient, it emerged between 13-11 billion years ago.[102]

But this was only the beginning.

Stars had also gathered towards the Galaxy's center called the 'bulge.' This formed around 10 billion years ago.[103] As new stars kept igniting between 13-10 billion years ago, the Galaxy was highly luminous and burned with fiery frenzy. Adding even more to its effulgence were the frequent supernovae. Today, such explosions are comparatively rare. But when they occur, they can release as much energy as our Sun releases over its entire lifespan of billions of years. As you saw, they can be so bright they outshine the luminosity of the entire host galaxy.

That's today. Some studies show that supernovae at earlier times may have been even brighter.[104] Imagine, then, the brilliance of our Galaxy 13-10 billion years ago!

And it wasn't a miming game, either. You may have heard that sound doesn't travel in a vacuum. That is true. But it does travel where there is a medium, for instance, interstellar gas. Another example is the body of a star. Particularly a massive star turning into a supernova. The star generates sonic shock waves from within its

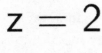

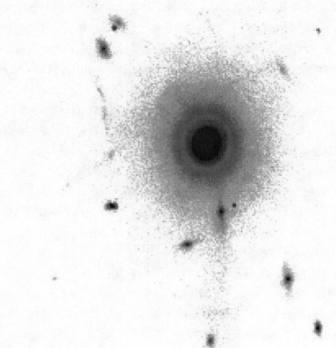

Fig 3.3. Computer-simulated image of a spiral galaxy when it was about 3 billion years old. It is composed of hundreds of stellar streams falling towards each other in loops, eventually merging to form a disk and halo. Image credit: Marie Martig, Center for Astrophysics and Supercomputing, Swinburne University of Technology, Hawthorn, Victoria 3122, Australia.

core. These thunderclaps are amongst the most energetic events in the universe. The colossal clangs can rip the original star generating clouds apart.[105]

In this way, brilliant, burning, exploding stars emerged in trillions all across the universe. They initially gathered into small groups that collided and merged with neighboring ones.[106] As these

Fig 3.4. A very early proto-galaxy would have comprised thousands more stellar streams like these falling towards each other in loops and eventually merging to form a halo and disk. (Artist's conception.)

throngs rushed towards each other, they stretched into elongated arms. These passed through and then fell back towards each other forming thousands of streams and loops. Some scientists have likened this very early appearance of galaxies to jumbles of starry spaghetti strands and pasta shells.[107] (Figure 3.3 and 3.4)

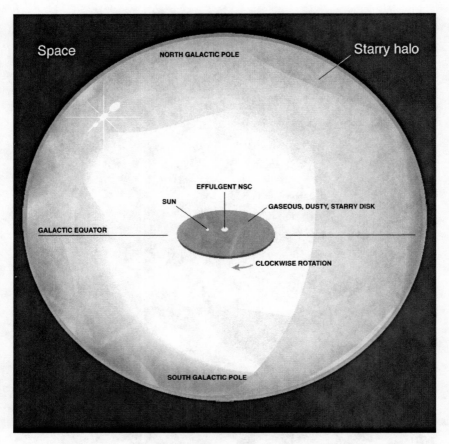

Fig 3.5. Schematic view of our Galaxy. Notice the spheroidal halo of stars. Today it's very dim, but the starry, gaseous disk at its center shines brightly. Its central position delineates the galactic equator and 'divides' the Galaxy into an upper and lower hemisphere.

The universe's first galaxies were born. Billions of them. Most of their stellar streams, combined with numerous gas clouds, eventually coalesced into huge spheroidal star systems like our own Milky Way Galaxy with an outer starry halo and commonly, a disk of gas, dust, and brilliant stars at their center. At the center of such disks is the effulgent bulge. (Figure 3.5 and 3.9) But that wasn't the end. They continued to grow and fatten as they swallowed each other and nearby clouds.

Our Milky Way Galaxy began very small, and grew ... and grew. In fact, even after 13 billion years, our Galaxy is still attracting new material and growing today.[108]

During all the original frenzy and fire, however, two extraordinary things were happening. The appearance of masses of dust and water.

WATER, WATER EVERYWHERE

Have you ever wondered where water comes from? Maybe you thought it emerged on our planet. The truth is quite different.

It comes from distant stars.

How do they produce it? Scientists know that stars produce oxygen and it reacts with the hydrogen in the vicinity.

Result: water.

Importantly, billions of years ago when the universe and galaxies were young, the amount wasn't trivial. It was abundant.[109] Water swirled in galaxies at least 12 billion years ago[110] and was copious in many dusty galaxies 9 billion years ago.[111]

The water flowing through your taps, the water you drink, the water in our rivers and oceans, is all a gift from the stars. Life-progenitors and thirst-quenchers of the universe, early stars began manufacturing the lifeblood of innumerable creatures on our planet, including ourselves.

ROCKY EARTHS

You have seen that many early stars exploded as supernovae. A hallmark of supernovae is the creation of 'dust.'

The dust beneath your feet and blowing in your backyard contains material that was once within a star. Stars are factories that forge the elements needed to form dust, including iron, silicon, carbon, and sulfur, at their cores. When a star ends its life and puffs off its outer shells, or if the star explodes, these elements are released into space, where they condense into dust. Eventually, some of that dust clumps together to build rocky planets like our Earth.

For the first few billion years after stars began to form, much of the dust gathered into enormous clouds. Recently, scientists discovered there was so much, early galaxies were *filled* with it. About 10-11 billion years ago, dust so engulfed some of them that light from their stars was rendered all but invisible.[112] It turns out that early supernovae were efficient dust-generating machines. Just one exploding star could release enough dust to build 10,000 Earths.[113]

Now consider this. Our Galaxy had an abundance of water, too. The dust and water would later come together to build planet Earths around stars like our Sun.

How many Earths do scientists predict?

About 45 *billion*.[114]

Indeed, scientists think Earth-like planets are very common in our Galaxy. As many as 40-60 percent of Sun-like stars could have them.[115] Moreover, 75 percent of these Earth-like planets may be older than ours. They would range from around 5-7 billion years old. The rest would be either older or younger than this.[116]

Comparatively, our Sun, Earth, Moon, and various planets of our solar system are quite young. The Sun evolved 4.6 billion years ago and the Earth and Moon evolved around 4.5 billion years ago. Incidentally, because we're currently moving through a star forming region of the Galaxy, many of the stars around us are even younger. The majority of stars we see with the naked eye at night were born after our Sun.[117]

Hundreds of planets have already been discovered. But they are mostly enormous, gaseous, and very far away. Recently, however, the very first near *Earth-sized* planets were discovered.[118] Immensely important discoveries in themselves, they're even more significant because the planets are very close by. Just a few dozen light years away, finding them so near to our own indicates how common Earth-sized planets must be. The implications for extraterrestrial life are huge. Wherever conditions on Earth-sized planets are favorable, many scientists believe plant and other life will almost certainly have appeared – even on planets older than ours.[119]

A WHIRLPOOL OF GAS AND STARS

You just witnessed the ancient conception of our Galaxy. The first structure to come together was a spheroidal or ball-like halo of stars. At its center were assembling other stars merging into a blazing bulge. For the first three billion years, these dominated the scene with many new stars entering the drama. But as some stars disappeared after exploding, and as others aged and new ones formed less frequently, another astounding structure was forming.

Within the halo and around the bulge, right on center stage, was a brilliant, gorgeous disk of stars – a magnificent revolving wheel!

How did this majestic and dazzling disk get there?

About 10 billion years ago, a rotating disk of hydrogen gas settled at the center of our Galaxy.[120] More and more gas from various sources merged with it and it grew broader, denser, and thicker.[121] Within it, a thinner disk also evolved. It gave birth to many stars and comprises the luminous disk visible today. The major portion of this disk formed about 8 billion years ago.[122] All in all, the entire disk formed between 10-8 billion years ago.

Truly breathtaking is its appearance. Its stars illuminate a spiral, whirlpool pattern. This is because the disk is gravitationally unstable and spinning faster inside than out. This and other complex processes create sweeping arms of gas, dust, and stars.[123] (Figures 3.6, 3.7, 3.8, 3.9) In fact, ninety percent of all the stars in our entire Galaxy are situated within this highly populated disk. It's the site of large volumes of gas and new star formation.[124] It's therefore very bright. Nearly all the stars you see with the naked eye in the sky, including our Sun, belong to this disk. They are young and local to us.[125]

One of the most striking features of the galactic disk is that it slowly rotates. Like a graceful ballerina, its sweeping spiral arms turn elegantly. Of course, the movement of these stars cannot be detected with the naked eye. Only careful observation with powerful telescopes can reveal their clockwise motion around the center.

Even our Pole star (Polaris), which seems fixed in the northern sky, travels clockwise in this disk.

Though the galactic motion of the stars is not visible with the naked eye, if you look for a while at the night stars they *do* appear to be moving. All these stars seem to travel from east to west, in a *counter*clockwise direction around the Pole star. This movement isn't real. It's only apparent or 'diurnal' (daily). (Figure 3.10)

The movement is caused by our Earth revolving on its axis. Like the Sun, it is not the stars that are revolving around the Earth, but the Earth itself that is revolving. The reason the Pole star appears not to be moving is because it lies right above the Earth's axis.

There is one more important location I would like to take you to. It's at our Galaxy's center. Called the Nuclear Stellar Cluster (NSC), it's a tiny ball of young, giant stars with a multimillion solar mass black hole at their center.[126] The young, giant stars make the NSC super-luminous. However, there is a huge amount of dust and gas floating between it and Earth. This renders it invisible.

Fig 3.6. The Whirlpool Galaxy (M51). Viewed face on. It's a spiral galaxy similar to our Milky Way. Spiral galaxies are often described as 'whirlpools' or 'pinwheels' in space. Image credit: NASA, ESA, S. Beckwith (STScI), and The Hubble Heritage Team STScI/AURA.

Fig 3.7. The Pinwheel Galaxy (M101). Viewed face on. Image credit: ESA & NASA.

Fig 3.8. NGC 1232. A spiral galaxy. Image credit: ESO.

Fig 3.9. NGC 4565, the Needle Galaxy. Viewed from side. It's a spiral galaxy. Note the central bulge and thinness of its dusty disk. Image credit: ESO.

Fig 3.10. A naked-eye view of the stars at night. The streaks indicate their blurred motion around the Pole star. Arrows indicate their observable *counter*-clockwise motion.

Luckily, our Sun is in motion and we're slowly climbing out of the hazy disk. In millions of years' time, our descendants will enjoy a spectacular view of this tiny, but luminous center.[127]

The universe seems to love constructing picturesque galaxies like our own. Spiral galaxies are plentiful. Some scientists think the disks of these galaxies are the most probable location for the existence of life. In our Galaxy, certainly, the disk is where our solar system resides, with all the diversity of life we see on our blue-green planet.

Lastly, you might ask, 'Will this Galaxy, our beautiful illuminated home, one day end? Or will it shine forever?

Unfortunately, its stars will eventually run out of fuel. They will die out. All good things pass, it seems. This should give us incentive to respect what we have. To treasure and nurture it. Our

Earth, Sun, and Galaxy will one day go dark. This Galaxy, this oasis in the Sahara of space is a gift, a consequence of the Big Bang – the ultimate free lunch.

Gratefully, the end of our Galaxy won't arrive for a long time. Scientists have given a rough estimate. The Milky Way will go dark in about 100 trillion years. This is when the last of its longest shining stars will have expended their fuel and finally sputtered out.[128]

The same scenario is likely to apply to all galaxies throughout the universe, since they were created around the same time. After 100 trillion years, all stars everywhere in the universe will die and the cosmos will gradually fade to darkness again.

CAN *ANY*, LET ALONE ALL these modern discoveries converge with descriptions given by the ancient Yogis and Israelites? Could they have known all this about our Galaxy? Could they have known there are numerous others, too?

Like the previous section on the Ancient Global Extinction, this section also bears fundamental similarities with Genesis. The descriptions of both traditions are marvelous and throw a lot of much needed light on each other. Each narrative complements the other. Understanding one, illuminates the other. You will be amazed.

Let us first take a close look at descriptions of a fascinating cosmic structure I introduced you to earlier. The Yogis called it a *brahmanda*.

They often used this word meaning 'Brahma's Egg' to describe enormous and innumerable 'cosmic eggs' or 'cocoons' speeding through limitless space. These cocoons were resplendent with light when they first arose. Today, many of them contain a disk of stars and planets that revolve around a minute, resplendent center. Indeed, our Sun, its planets, and all the stars in the night sky belong to a revolving disk of gas within one such cocoon. The cocoons are not exactly egg-shaped, though. The eggs are described as 'bubble-like,' that is, spheroidal. The egg is a metaphor used to illustrate the fact that all life incubates and lives within these enormous star systems. Each cosmic egg represents a habitable locale in the infinite emptiness of space.

This ancient description sounds extraordinarily close to modern science! Initially, our egg was 'golden' or effulgent. The ancients referred to this structure metaphorically as the *hiranya garbha* (Golden Womb or Egg). It was as 'resplendent as the Sun.' Also striking is the Sanskrit root *bruh* from which the term *brahmanda* derives. *Bruh* means *'to grow.'* It seems the cosmic egg grew from small to huge, just like our Milky Way Galaxy.

In the previous two sections you saw 40 correspondences with science. Following, you will see that there are still many more. The five sections in this book present 20+20+42+18+17=117 convergences in total. How can there be so many coherent convergences with modern science by accident?

Three misunderstood metaphors

In earlier translations of the Yoga Literature, this hugely important word – *brahmanda* – has often been translated as 'universe.' It turns out to be a mistake of astronomical proportions. Literally. Misgauging this word distorted everything else the Yogis said about the world and its creation. The 'universe' they described seemed to have little in common with the universe known to science. As such, everything they said was discarded as mythology, fantasy, and fiction.

On the other hand, if *brahmanda* is translated as *galaxy*, everything falls into place magnificently. The mosaic comes together meaningfully. In fact, as you will soon see, the convergences between *brahmanda* and galaxy are stupendous.

Another word that has been misgauged is *prithivi*. It's often translated as 'earth' – planet Earth, the land we reside on. In the symbolism of the Yoga Literature, it seems the Yogis may be speaking of a flat earth. But this is a mistake as immense as the previous.

Asking the right question is half the challenge solved. Here, the question is: might the Yogis' use of the word earth refer to something other than its modern use, planet Earth?

The answer is a resounding *yes*. They clearly described the earth-*prithivi* as fiery like a revolving disk of burning coal, bathed in golden light, immensely broad, and extending as far as the stars. It's a structure of cosmic extent. Yes, it's flat. But it doesn't refer to the planet beneath our feet.

Take a look. Does the earth look like a disk of burning coal? Does it extend as far as the stars? In this context, the ancient description makes little sense. But when instead of (flat planet) earth, it's compared to our Galaxy's flat disk of gas, dust, planets, and stars, all the passages sing like a symphony. In fact, the Yogis stated clearly that the word earth is not limited to planet Earth. It refers to *wherever* in the *brahmanda*-Galaxy there is land that can be walked on. That means all rocky planets!

The same issue has arisen in translations of the Bible. Here, too, the word 'earth' is sometimes used in cosmic contexts. It does not refer to planet Earth or the land beneath our feet, but to a cosmic, earthy disk astronomical in size. More and more scholars are coming to realize this.[129]

Let me introduce you to one more misjudged word: *padma*. It means lotus. (Figure 3.11) This word is also mentioned in clear cosmic contexts. It's a metaphor that refers to our entire *brahmanda*-Galaxy and often the starry disk within it. It's absurd when some scholars suggest ancient Yogis naively believed creation began with the emergence of a real lotus flower hanging in space. As I showed earlier, ancient people were every bit as ra-

Fig 3.11. The radiant lotus flower (not to be confused with the lily) has a conical central seed cup. The lotus was a mystical symbol of our Galaxy.

tional as we are. Descriptions of lotus flowers blooming in infinite space are obvious metaphors and deserve closer inspection.

In fact, choosing lotus for our Galaxy was probably the most excellent of the ancient symbols. Native to India, the lotus is exquisite. It comes in various colors, usually shades of pink or white. In the Yoga Literature, it's described as 'golden' or 'shining.' The flower is also broad, often spanning eight inches or more. As well as relating the *brahmanda*-Galaxy to the lotus flower, the Yogis sometimes compared the *brahmanda*-Galaxy's flat starry disk to the lotus *leaf* which is also flat and circular. A very appropriate symbol indeed.

Another novel characteristic of the flower is that it grows in water. Usually found in shallow ponds, it grows from the muddy floor upwards towards the light. Eventually it emerges from the water in the morning and blossoms gloriously.

Accordingly, the ancient Yogis likened the flower to an enormous, cosmic disk of stars and habitable worlds (*loka*, or planets) that emerged from a watery environ at the dawn of creation. It looked golden and luminescent like the morning Sun. Like the flat, round lotus leaf, it's a wonderful metaphor of our dazzling starry disk mixed with earthy planets emerging in a watery, dusty galaxy billions of years ago!

Let us take a look at all these metaphors and their numerous correspondences with our Milky Way Galaxy. You will also see clear correspondences with the Big Bang.

Then we will move on to Genesis.

Come.

Key Points to Remember

1. The entire observable universe began in a tiny seed.
2. Time was intertwined with that primordial seed.
3. The seed expanded.
4. Space expanded.
5. Elementary particles formed.
6. They formed within a second.
7. Primordial matter burst forth in all directions.
8. It occurred all of a sudden, in a flash.
9. Primordial matter gravitationally collapsed into a network of filaments.
10. Galaxies developed on this network.
11. Our Galaxy of stars (and other galaxies) emerged from darkness.
12. It formed from the primordial matter.
13. It grew.
14. It grew gradually.
15. It grew by attracting matter from around it.
16. It was like a ball of fire because it comprised of stars.
17. It became effulgent.
18. The stars gathered into a spheroidal or ball-shaped halo.
19. There was water.
20. There was dust.
21. Stars formed within the disk of gas that the Galaxy accreted.

22. It formed within the starry spheroid.
23. The disk revolves.
24. It looks like a whirlpool.
25. It's a great wheel of gas and dust.
26. Billions of stars including the stars and planets we see in the night sky revolve within this wheel.
27. At their center is an object called the NSC at whose center is a multimillion solar mass 'black hole.'
28. Even the Sun orbits it.
29. Even the 'fixed' Pole star orbits it.
30. All these orbit it in a clockwise direction.
31. The central NSC is minute.
32. Like other clusters, it's highly luminous.
33. It's spheroidal.
34. The disk has an attractive pull.
35. Within the Galaxy, it contains the highest concentration of earthy, rock-forming elements.
36. The entire Galaxy attracts elements towards it.
37. The disk is the location of our Sun and humankind.
38. The Galaxy experiences explosive events such as supernovae.
39. There is associated extreme effulgence of light.
40. The Galaxy's halo and bulge developed 13-10 billion years ago.
41. Its disk with Earth-sized planets is estimated to have formed around 7-5 billion years ago.
42. The longest shining stars of our Galaxy will shine for another 100 trillion years.

WHAT THE ANCIENT YOGIS KNEW

Material creation in the form of perceivable [things],
arises from a Dot (*bindu*).

Pancharatra, Ahirbudhnya Samhita 16.81-83, 88-90, 16.94

**Our material universe arose from a minute point, a dot,
like the Big Bang.**

Thus this creation of primordial matter ...
[appeared] at first unpremeditatedly,
as lightning appears.

Vayu Purana 4.80cdef; Markandeya Purana 45.73; Brahmanda Purana 1.1.3.37

As the [vast] banyan [tree] rises from the [tiny] seed
at the appearance of the germ and expands,
so does the world
from [the Lord] at [the time of] creation.

Vishnu Purana 1.12.65-66

The tiny seed expands to create the world.

At the time of creation, the disk of earth
(*prithivinu mandal* or disk of the world) ...
was in the form of a supreme particle
(*paramanu rupa*).[130]

Vachanamruta, Gadhada II.64

At the time of creation, our world was in the form
of a tiny fundamental particle.

Primordial Time
was in the form of a supreme particle.

Vedras, Nihspruhi Vartman[131]

Time was woven with the primordial fundamental particle.

[In the beginning of creation]
the quintessence of space arises,
which is emptiness.

[Creation] shines forth vehemently
and within a second (*kshana*)

becomes the elementary particles of Gas,
spreading out into wind.

Then, brilliance comes into being.
These are the elementary particles
of Light.

That – is the origin of the growth of the Sun and fire –
and is the cause of vision ... .

[Then] water appears ... then earth.

This is the essence of the cosmic egg (*bhugolaka* or *brahmanda*)
that is to be, the foundation of everything.

Yoga Vasishta 3.12.9, 18-27; Bhagavata Purana 2.5.26-30; Manu Smriti 1.70-80

[The Lord] who is the wind
by which dances the vine that is primordial matter,
which is born in space,
has cosmic eggs for its good fruits.
(Figures 3.12 and 4.4)

Yoga Vasishta 3.5.17

Primordial matter across the universe
appeared like the network of a creeper plant.
It developed 'fruits' upon it in the form of starry *brahmandas*.

Fig 3.12. Berries forming on the network of a creeper plant. Ancient Yogis used this analogy to describe *brahmandas* forming on a vine or network of primordial matter in space.

When this [world] was lightless and dark,
surrounded on all sides by darkness,
a single, huge egg came into being.

Markandeya Purana 101.21

That [seed] became a golden egg
equal in brilliance to the Sun.

Manu Smriti 1.9

The cosmic egg has the nature
of luminaries [stars and planets].

Kurma Purana 2.46.13

The cosmic egg consists of stars and planets.

That great egg grew from the elements gradually
and uniformly like a bubble in water.

Vishnu Purana 1.2.50cd, 53, 54cd-56

There that huge egg lying in the water,

like a bubble in water,
gradually attained growth from the elements.

Markandeya Purana 45.61-73, Vayu Purana 4.67

That eggshell lay soulless in the water
of the ocean for a full [divine] millennium.
Then the Lord inhabited it.

From his navel (or center) a lotus (*padma*)
came into being,
widely shining like a thousand Suns,
the abode of the entire collective of beings.

Bhagavata Purana 3.20.14-16

A brightly shining 'lotus' arose at the center of the egg.
It was the region where all life would appear.
(Here, the Lord manifests as the First Avatar in a cosmic form. See Workshop
4 and Section 5.)

Sleeping for a thousand quadruple-ages (*chaturyuga*) ...
he [the Lord] saw the worlds
incorporated in his own body.

As his sight was fixed on the subtle matter,

the very fine matter inside him ...
broke forth from the region of his navel ... .

That lotus bud rose up suddenly,
illuminating that huge water with its own brilliance
like a Sun born of itself.

Bhagavata Purana 3.8.12-14

The shining 'lotus' appeared suddenly from the center of the Lord
after one thousand quadruple-ages of rest. (Workshops 4 and 5)
It was the region where all the inhabitable worlds appeared.

This entire world – the Sun, the Moon,
along with the constellations ... and Gas,
and everything that is this world and that is not,
is established in that egg.

Brahmanda Purana 1.1.3.29-38

[Student speaking to Yogi:] You have said that
the specific extent of the disk of the earth
is [as far as] where the Sun shines
and where the Moon is seen
along with the hosts of luminaries [stars and planets].

... evenly round like a lotus leaf.

Bhagavata Purana 5.16.1, 5

All 'earth' extends as far as all the luminaries (planets and stars) in the sky
in a disk-like formation within the egg.

Whatever manner of thing consisting of earth
there is that can be walked on,
that is called the earthy world.

Vishnu Purana 2.7.16

Wherever in the egg there is land that can be walked on, that is called 'earth.'

The disk of the earth ... is as much
as the sphere in the sky,
which is for the attachment of the stars.

Matsya Purana 124.19-20ab; Brahmanda Purana 1.2.21.17

The disk-like 'earth' is as broad as the disk-like region of stars.

The disk of stars,
which like a swarm of mosquitoes ...
appears to rotate like a whirlpool ... .

In it there are objects of various forms:
some greatly luminous [stars], some of little luminosity,
and some without luminosity [planets], which are illuminated.

Yoga Vasishta 6.2.187.24-25

This disk is the wheel of the world,
whose majesty is famed in scripture ... .

Because it turns about, eternally fading and blazing up,
like a whirlwind that is a disk of embers,
therefore it is referred to as a disk.

Because at the beginning of creation
the wheel was created very wide,
it is designated by the name 'wideness' [*prithvi*].

This wheel, rests in golden light ... .

It is surrounded by water ...
surrounded by space ... ."

THE BIG BANG AND OUR GALAXY

Shiva Purana (Kailasha Samhita).15.39-44

**The disk-like earth looks like a whirlwind of blazing embers.
(It does not resemble planet Earth.)**

This [earth] with its villages,
cities and mountains came into being ...
like a ripe walnut with its coat.

Yoga Vasishta 3.30.14

**Planet Earth is not flat. It is round like a walnut.
(In contrast, the disk of the world is flat.)**

The Sun ... ceaselessly circles Meru clockwise,
and so does the Moon along with the stars
and the Gas.

Mahabharata 6.7.14

**The effulgent Meru is at the center of the starry disk in the cosmic egg,
not the Earth, Sun, or Pole star.**

With the Sun, the Pole star [too] revolves.

Brahmanda Purana 1.2.22.77-78

The Pole star alone revolves at the summit of Mount Meru ...
circling it clockwise.

Brahmanda Purana 1.2.23.108

[At the center of the *brahmanda*] is Meru,
the round golden mountain,
having the fresh blaze of the Sun
like a smokeless fire.

Mahabharata 6.7.8cd-9ab

The effulgent structure at the center of the cosmic egg is spherical in shape.

Mount Meru ...

has a round-shaped circumference.

Brahmanda Purana 1.2.15.17

[In the cosmic egg]
that part [consisting] of earthy substances
is situated like a lotus leaf.

[The other elements] rush toward that as children
[rush] toward [their] mother.

Therefore objects rush, like thirsty people to water,
toward that great body
called a cosmic egg that is nearer.

Yoga Vasishta 6.2.80.52-53

The cosmic egg and the earthy areas within it have the property of attracting
nearby objects towards them. (This is the principle of gravity.)
The earthy parts are laid out in a disk-like area.

All these descriptions correspond closely to our Galaxy and its
creation from the Big Bang.

Is it an accident?

How did the Yogis know the entire universe emerged from a
tiny point, shining forth vehemently like a flash of lightning? How

did they know gas appeared within a second? (Workshop 3) How did they know primordial matter resembled a vine spread across the whole of space? How did they know immense star systems (*brahmandas*) evolved on it? How did they know they contain starry disks? How did they know the disk in our system rotates? How did they know its stars, including the Pole star which appears fixed to the naked eye, rotate clockwise around a luminous center?

How much closer to a description of the Big Bang and our universe can you get?

Are all these descriptions just a coincidence? Is it possible the Yogis gave them whimsically and by inconceivable chance they were all correct? Can a hurricane really assemble a space shuttle from a scrap heap?

No. It's unconscionable. In light of the extraordinary descriptions the same Yogis gave of deep-sea volcanoes, hydrothermal vents, and the Permian-Triassic extinctions, these convergences concerning the Big Bang and our universe make sense and are hardly surprising, though they are still extraordinary.

Unfortunately, as you saw earlier, it has been the approach of some scholars to depict ancient people, particularly non-Greeks, as simpletons. They were non-thinkers. They were naive. They blindly believed whatever they saw with their eyes. A consequence of this approach is that some skeptics portray these ancients as people who merely stared at the night sky, saw that stars appear to revolve around the Earth and Pole star, and thought that this is the way the world truly is. What they saw at night was their universe. It was as it appeared. Nothing larger. Nothing contrary. (Figure 3.10, p. 115[132])

Is this claim acceptable?

Again, no. Contrary to it, you have seen that the description the Yogis gave of the Sun and stars on four counts *repudiates* what you see with the naked eye. The Yogis said:

1. The motion of the stars is *clockwise*.
2. Even the Pole star is in *clockwise* motion.
3. The motion of the Sun is *clockwise*.
4. The Sun, Pole star, and innumerable other stars, all revolve in a clockwise direction around a tiny, invisible, but effulgent center called the Meru.

It was the invisible, resplendent Meru that was the center of the Yogis' cosmic egg, not the Pole star. I am happy to say that some other researchers have realized this, too.[133] The Yogis' cosmos was different from what we see in the night sky, but similar to what we see with advanced telescopes.

But what about the timeline? Numbers are even harder to guess. If these Yogis in their loincloths were making it all up, it would be impossible to give the correct timeline. Only modern science can do this. The answer, you saw is 13-10 billion years ago for the formation of the halo and bulge, and about 7-5 billion years ago for the formation of its disk with habitable Earth-like planets.

What timeline did the Yogis give? 20,000 years ago? 57 trillion years ago? No.

They gave 14.9-10.6 billion years ago for the egg-cocoon and 6.3 billion years ago for the Earth-like habitable worlds! These periods converge with modern science. This is truly amazing. (Workshops 4 and 5)

One last thing.

Some people may still think this was all some sort of lucky guesswork about the past. If the Yogis really knew when our *brahmanda*-Galaxy and starry disk formed, surely they should also know when it will all end, when the lights will die out. Science estimates it will happen after roughly 100 trillion years.

Did the Yogis give a life span for the egg?

Yes. They said the *brahmanda*-Galaxy will die at the end of the life span of Brahma.

How far in the future is that? 6,000 years? 5 billion years? No. 155 *trillion* years. (Workshop 6)

This is yet another superb convergence with science.

Such knowledge of our Earth and Milky Way without the support of modern science is impossible to acquire. Yet ancient Yogis (and Israelites) clearly possessed this intricate information.

Remember, even the most powerful of intellectual thinkers and speculators across millennia from Plato to Newton couldn't access this knowledge. In fact, even scientists today would not be able to derive all this information if it was not for the use of complex mathematical theorems and powerful modern instruments. So its existence in ancient spiritual texts is enthralling. The new convergences cannot be ignored and beg an explanation.

But there are very few options available. In fact, the only alternative and rational answer – however much disliked by skeptics – is the *spiritual* one. And indeed, it is the very answer given by the ancient sages and yogis themselves! The inner spiritual path that led them to discover our universe and describe it in so much authentic detail, also led them to God.

Can and should we take their word for it?

Can all this complex, detailed, and coherent knowledge of deep-sea volcanoes, hydrothermal vents, an ancient worldwide extinction, our Galaxy, and creation of our universe from a tiny point really arise by chance? Can it be a fluke as incredible as a hurricane blowing through a junkyard and constructing a new space shuttle? You decide.

We will now take a look at the really big picture of our universe. We know today that it doesn't consist of just one galaxy, our own, or only a few, but hundreds of billions of them.

Did the Yogis and Israelites know this, too? Could they have known much more? How much more?

During my research, this is what I found.

Workshop 3

Yogis stated that elementary components of gas evolved within a second or '1 kshana' after creation began. How long is a kshana? The Yogis calibrated time differently from the way we're familiar today. They divided it according to the following method.

30 Muhurtas = 1 day and night (24 hours); 30 Kalas = 1 Muhurta;
30 Kashtas = 1 Kala; 15 Nimeshas = 1 Kashta.
(*Markandeya Purana* 43.23)

3 Nimeshas = 1 Kshana
(*Bhagavata Purana* 3.11.17)

Therefore 1 Kshana = 0.64 seconds.

Workshop 4

Let us analyze three timelines given by the Yogis concerning when the egg formed.

You saw earlier that they called a single day in the life of the demiurge Brahma a 'kalpa.' This day is followed by night which is also a period called a kalpa. 1 kalpa equals the immense period of 4.32 billion years. In the literature regarding creation, we find the Yogis describe only the very first day and then the last four consecutive days and nights of Brahma's life till now.[134] The process of creation the Yogis described goes like this:

In the beginning, God (Isha) created the demiurge Brahma. That celebrated eon is called the Brahma Kalpa. Then, after a series of metaphysical creations, God created the basic physical elements. First emerged Space (akasha). From this emerged Gas (vayu). From Gas emerged Fire (or Light, tejas). From Fire, emerged Water (jala). And after Water emerged Earth (or dust, prithivi). During this first phase of creation, the first Avatar of God called 'Purusha'[135] guided the above elements and caused them to form into a huge, fiery, spheroidal cosmic cocoon, the brahmanda. Like the thousands of kalpas between it and that of Brahma's birth, this kalpa wherein the physical elements emerged and created an egg, is unnamed. I have arbitrarily named it the 'Elemental Kalpa.'[136] (*When* this physical phase of creation began and how long it lasted is not mentioned, either. However, since a period of one kalpa is definitely the theme we see throughout consequent kalpas which are consecutive with it, it is reasonable to assume it was a period of 1 kalpa, too. Nevertheless, it is an assumption.) Purusha also evolved masses of water. The egg became his physical body which he pervaded as its 'soul.' With this cosmic body he lay on those cosmic waters in meditative rest for a period of 1 kalpa, or 4.32 billion years (*Bhagavata Purana 3.8.12*). This kalpa is also unnamed. I have arbitrarily named it the 'Purusha Kalpa.' After this eon, Purusha stirred and a resplendent structure began to spread out from the center of his cosmic body. Named the 'Padma' or Lotus [flower] by the Yogis, it evolved into the fiery, revolving disk of the world. The new eon was named the Padma Kalpa. (*Bhagavata Purana 3.8.12-14 & 3.11.35*) Thereafter ensued the current eon, named the Varaha Kalpa. (*Bhagavata Purana 3.8.12-14 & 3.11.36*)

Briefly, then, the ancients describe the creation of the cosmic egg as having passed through *four consecutive* kalpas. Three kalpas (Elemental, Purusha, and Padma), each of 4.32 billion years duration, have wholly passed. We are currently in the 4th kalpa (Varaha), in its 7th manvantara of which 27 Maha Yugas, 1 Satya, 1 Treta, 1 Dvapara, and part Kali have passed. (*Kurma Purana* 1.5.26 and *Bhagavata Purana* 3.11.29-38)

We know the egg began forming during the Elemental Kalpa and 'incubated' during the Purusha Kalpa wherein the Lord rested for 1,000 chatur yugas, an entire eon. This means the eon during which the egg formed was the Elemental Kalpa and it began:

Part Kali + 1 Dvapara + 1 Treta + 1 Satya + 27 Maha Yugas of Vaivasvata + 6 Manvantaras of Varaha + Padma + Purusha + Elemental =

5,000 + 864,000 + 1,296,000 + 1,728,000 + (27 x 4.32 million) + (6 x 308.5 million) + 4.32 billion + 4.32 billion + 4.32 billion

= 14,931,533,000 years ago

and ended:

Part Kali + 1 Dvapara + 1 Treta + 1 Satya + 27 Maha Yugas of Vaivasvata + 6 Manvantaras of Varaha + Padma + Purusha =

5,000 + 864,000 + 1,296,000 + 1,728,000 + (27 x 4.32 million) + (6 x 308.5 million) + 4.32 billion + 4.32 billion

= 10,611,533,000 years ago

This is roughly between about 14.9-10.6 billion years ago.

Workshop 5

The disk with inhabitable worlds (planets) began forming immediately after the Purusha Kalpa at the beginning of the Padma Kalpa. This means the beginning of this eon in which the inhabitable disk formed began:

Part Kali + 1 Dvapara + 1 Treta + 1 Satya + 27 Maha Yugas of Vaivasvata
+ 6 Manvantaras of Varaha + Padma =

5,000 + 864,000 + 1,296,000 + 1,728,000 + (27 x 4.32 million)
+ (6 x 308.5 million) + 4.32 billion

= 6,291,533,000 years ago

This is roughly 6.3 billion years ago.

Workshop 6

Brahma's life span lasts for 100 years. Each year consists of twelve months, each month thirty days and nights long, and each day and each night (both called a kalpa) 4.32 billion years long. This yields a total of 360 'days' per year. He has already completed the first half of his life span and has begun the first day of its latter half (parardha). (*Bhagavata Purana 3.11.32* and *Vachanamruta, Bhugol Khagol*) This means his total life span is:

(1 Day + 1 Night) x 30 Days x 12 Months x 100 Years
(4.32 billion + 4.32 billion) x 30 x 12 x 100 =

311,040,000,000,000 = or roughly 311 trillion years.

His remaining life span is therefore:

(Total life span / 2) - Part Kali - 1 Dvapara - 1 Treta - 1 Satya
- 27 Maha Yugas of Vaivasvata - 6 Manvantaras of Varaha =

(311,040,000,000,000 / 2) - 5,000 - 864,000 - 1,296,000 - 1,728,000
- (27 x 4.32 million) - (6 x 308.5 million) =

155,518,028,500,000 = or roughly 155 trillion years.

Section

THE LIMITLESS UNIVERSE

HOW ARE GALAXIES SPREAD across our universe? What does the overall layout look like? How did it get this way?

Initially, scientists believed the majority of galaxies must be spread uniformly across the universe. The notion was reversed in the 1980s. New maps and photographs felled the scientific community: The universe contains great arrays of galaxies gathered in hierarchies of groups, clusters, and superclusters. About 50 galaxies is called a group, but a cluster could have thousands. (Figure 4.1) These in turn form grand superclusters some of which comprise tens or even hundreds of thousands of galaxies spanning several hundred millions of light years across.[137]

The clusters and superclusters define a sponge-like network grouped in chains and filaments. They aren't spread uniformly but stretch around colossal regions of empty space. (Figure 4.2[138])

There are various types of galaxies, each beautiful, luminous, and huge. All are in motion and at various stages of growth. Some galaxies seem to be isolated. Others are gravitationally bound to a group. Attracted by their mutual gravitation, many are approaching

Fig 4.1. An energetic collision of galactic clusters. Image credit: NASA, ESA, CXC, M. Bradac (University of California, Santa Barbara), and S. Allen (Stanford University).

each other. Some, like ours and Andromeda, will clash and merge. Some are already in contact with one another. (Figure 4.3) Others contain very few stars making them appear hollow and dark.[139] Some are disintegrating. Much to the surprise of scientists, it was discovered that not all galaxies are ancient. Some are newly forming.[140]

Everything in our universe is in motion. Atoms, planets, stars, galaxies, and superclusters of galaxies. All are cavorting. Thus we

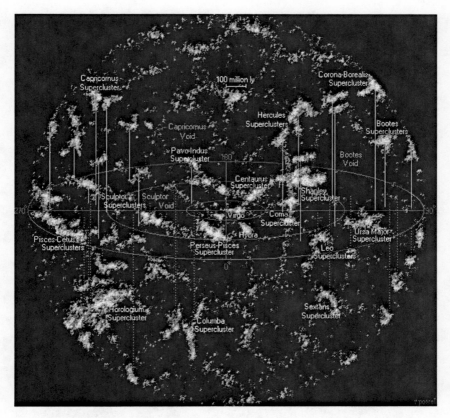

Fig 4.2. Innumerable galaxies are grouped and clustered into a network of filaments surrounding huge voids in space. In this image which represents just a minute portion of the universe, our Galaxy is located towards the center. Image credit: Richard Powell, 'The Universe Within 1 Billion Light Years; The Neighbouring Superclusters.'

have the cosmic dance of galaxies as they interact in a universe that has no special center. All directions and motions are relative.

Let us now see what the ancient Yogis said about their *brahmandas*. Are there many types? Do they interact? How are they arranged?

Importantly, does what they say correspond with science?

By now, you know the answer.

Fig 4.3. A triplet of galaxies: NGC 6769, NGC 6770, and NGC 6771. The upper two galaxies are in contact with one another. All three are interacting. Image credit: ESO.

Key Points to Remember

1. Galaxies exist in great assemblies.
2. Many are in superclusters of hundreds of thousands.
3. They all move through space.
4. There are various types of galaxies.
5. Some are newly forming.
6. Some are disintegrating.
7. Some are bound to each other.
8. Some are approaching each other.
9. Some are clashing.
10. Some are isolated, just flying through space.
11. Some are almost without stars, faintly emitting radio waves.
12. Huge parts of space are devoid of galaxies.
13. Innumerable galaxies have evolved.
14. There are other planet Earths associated with their respective Suns.
15. These Suns ultimately melt those Earths. (See Section 5)
16. Our Earth is a tiny ball, a seemingly insignificant speck in one such galaxy.
17. The universe has no center.
18. All directions and motions are relative.

WHAT THE ANCIENT YOGIS KNEW

And countless [cosmic] eggs of such [kinds] were born.

Agni Purana 120.16

It should be known that there are
thousands of ten millions of such eggs ...
horizontally, above and below.

Brahmanda Purana 1.2.19.158-159

Of such eggs there are thousands of thousands
or even myriads of them.

Pancharatra, Vishvaksena Samhita[141]

This huge egg shell
along with millions
of groups of [such] eggs ... . (Figures 3.12, 4.4)

Bhagavata Purana 3.11.39cd-40

Fig 4.4. Clusters of berries on a creeper plant. Ancient Yogis used this analogy to describe *brahmandas* grouped together like fruits on a vine of primordial matter branching across all directions in space. (Section 3)

There are, will be and have been innumerable worlds ... .
Heaps of hundred-thousands of cosmic eggs
are thus ever stationed ... .

They are like clusters of elementary particles of water
located in water
where the drift of spreading waves is unchecked.

Yoga Vasishta 6.2.170.1, 25

Infinite worlds rise and sink
in this great space ...
like the water of waves in the ocean.

It may be possible to count the dust-motes
jittering in the rays of the Sun,
but not the hosts of worlds ... .

As at the beginning of the rainy season
new and new throngs of mosquitoes
come into being fervently and disappear again,
so too these world-creations.

Yoga Vasishta 4.47.14, 16-17

As drunken spirits dance without ever seeing one another
in an enormous forest dense with terrible darkness,
so the numerous great worlds
flicker within the expansive supreme space.

Yoga Vasishta 3.30.32-34

Thus the worlds are in this tremendous space
that is the depository of the crowd of all substances.
Some [worlds] are in contact with one another,
some are not in contact with one another.

Yoga Vasishta 6.2.18.44

Some cosmic eggs are touching each other.

Lord Shiva wears a necklace
that is the collision of cosmic eggs.

Skanda Purana (Prabhasa Khanda) 7.19.32

Some cosmic eggs are clashing with each other.

The space is the network of worlds ... .

Yoga Vasishta 6.2.60.28

Cosmic eggs flicker into view like minute particles
in that supreme expanse.
In that expanse is everything,
from it is everything, it is everything.

In that ocean ... wavelets — called cosmic eggs
— eternally come and go.
Some, in the process of dissolution,
are empty within.

Like waves on water in the ocean,
they drift on in the ocean of emptiness.

Yoga Vasishta 3.30.15-18

The cosmic eggs are in motion.

Within some, the end of an aeon has [just] begun
with a gurgling roar — not heard, nor known by others ... .

In the earths of other [cosmic eggs?],
creation expands at the first beginning,
like the tiny germ within the husk of watered seeds.

In some, in the process of great dissolution,
the mountains have begun to melt

THE LIMITLESS UNIVERSE

from sunrays and lightning bolts,
like snowflakes in sunlight.

Some merely fall for an aeon
... till, dissolving.

Yoga Vasishta 3.30.19-22

There are other planet Earths.
They are associated with their own Suns.
Their Suns burn/melt those Earths. (Section 5)

There, having in a moment passed
the elemental coverings of the cosmic egg,
she [a Yogi] saw that supreme space
without measurement ... .

She saw [other] creations in cosmic eggs
with similar coverings,
glistening in their tens of millions
in space,
like dust motes in sunlight, like myriads of bubbles arising ...
in the great ocean of great space
whose water is the great emptiness.

Some cosmic eggs are falling down, some rising up,
some moving sideways,
others staying [relatively] fixed ... .

No such thing as up or down or coming
or going exists there [in space] like here,
[there is] only a certain different position,
and that [movement] is the movement
of a body from that [position].

What could be down, what could be up,
what could be sideways?

All objects rush to and fro in dependence.
What in [each] cosmic egg is the earthy part,
[towards] that is down, and [what is] otherwise is up.

Yoga Vasishta 3.30.1-34

All motions in the universe are relative.
(The universe has no center, the Cosmological Principle.)

The established succession in each cosmic egg is not universal.
Some have Brahma as the original Being,
some have Vishnu as the first protector of creation,
some have others as lords of offspring,
some have creatures without protectors.

Some have various lords of creation;
some are inhabited by animals [alone],
some are filled with a single ocean,
others are without population.

Some are unbroken like a body of rock;
some are inhabited by vermin alone;
some consist of divinities alone;
some are inhabited by men.

Some ever abound in darkness
and have creatures of such a nature;
some ever abound in light and have creatures of such a nature.

Some are filled with flies;
others have interiors ever empty,
with creatures whose essence is empty movement.

Others are filled with such [an alien] creation that in this world
they cannot even enter the imagination.

So expansive is the sky of these [cosmic eggs],
the great space,
that it could not be measured [even] by Vishnu and his like,
even were they to stride all their lives.

Yoga Vasishta 3.30.24-30

These are truly stunning descriptions of our universe and they converge exactly with modern science!

Let us examine one last splendid description.

A famous motif of the Yogis is that of the cosmic deity Nataraja – The King of Dancers. Nataraja is the cosmic form of Shiva (meaning 'auspiciousness') and is an ancient symbol of limitless space containing the dance of innumerable cosmic eggs or *brahmandas.*[142] In the shape of these *brahmandas,* the Nataraja performs this cosmic dance, or *tandava.* Its beginning depicts creation; its continuance, sustenance; its end, universal dissolution.

He is depicted as having four arms. In one hand he holds a drum. Its booming sound symbolizes the beginning of creation. In another hand, he holds a flame. It depicts the destruction of the Earth coming through the Sun. (See next Section.) A third hand grants solace. The fourth awards protection.[143]

There is a mystical tale related to this cosmic motif. The Yogis narrate a story of when a group of demons in our *brahmanda* tried to destroy the invincible Nataraja. After various failures they sent a dwarf demon called Apasmaara (Sanskrit: 'forgetfulness' or 'unheedfulness'). Nataraja destroyed it simply by stepping on its back.[144] Moral: No one can thwart the eternal cycle of creation and renewal, birth and death, without transcending to the spiritual. Unheedfulness spells misery. Annihilation of vanity and false ego leads to bliss.

Take a close look at Figure 4.5.

The upper picture is a modern image of nearby superclusters.[145] The dots in this pie-shaped segment of the universe comprise thousands of galaxies. Our Galaxy is at the segment's lowest point. Then look below at the ancient portrayal of the Nataraja, who symbolizes innumerable *brahmanda*-Galaxies, performing the cosmic dance. The image dates back at least a thousand years.[146] Apasmaara is depicted beneath the Nataraja's right foot.

Notice the overall likeness of our neighboring superclusters to Nataraja's limbs and clothing. Can you see the similarities? Across the whole universe, similar superclusters can be envisioned dancing everywhere. They are all parts of the cosmic Nataraja, the symbol of innumerable cosmic eggs, some clashing in his 'neck-

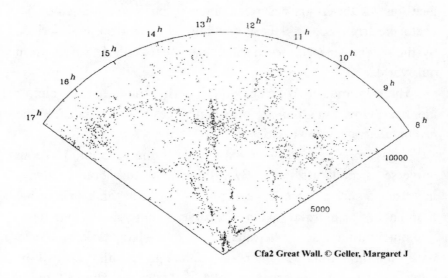

Cfa2 Great Wall. © Geller, Margaret J

Fig 4.5. The CfA2 Great Wall of galaxies (above) and an ancient image of the Nataraja below. Each dot in the upper pie-shaped segment represents a galaxy. Notice the overall likeness of the outline of our neighboring superclusters to Nataraja's legs, dangling waist ribbons, central body, head, and outstretched arms. Nataraja, who symbolizes the dance and clash of innumerable cosmic eggs represents the same dance of innumerable interacting galaxies in infinite space discovered by science.

lace' just as the Yogis described. Indeed, our Galaxy is close beneath the 'right foot' of these dancing galaxies, also as described
by the Yogis, since the demon beneath Nataraja's foot was from
our world.

The two images – one ancient, the other modern – are almost
identical! How can all these correspondences between galaxies and
brahmandas occur by accident?

Yogis millennia ago gave exactly the same description of our
universe as modern science. Everything they said about it emerging from a tiny point and its evolution from dancing primordial
filaments of primordial matter to evolve innumerable cosmic eggs
like ours with a starry spheroidal halo, inner starry disk, its clockwise rotation, luminous center, age of the egg and disk, and all the
other eggs grouped in great clusters of thousands, flying through
space in swarms, some receding and some clashing – all this and
much more, corresponds exactly with the Big Bang, our Milky
Way Galaxy, and its place amongst a network of innumerable superclusters of galaxies in our universe.

We can confidently conclude that the metaphorical
brahmanda-eggs the ancients spoke of are indeed the very same
'island universes' – the interacting, clustering, and clashing galaxies discovered by modern science. The total number of convergences with science, many of them numerical, is overwhelming:
sixty. Truly, it was not the ancients who didn't know what they were
talking about, but we who didn't know what *they* were talking
about.

We have covered a lot of ground – I should say universe – in
the last one hundred pages. Within them you have seen numerous
convergences of modern science and ancient spirituality. Out of all
this, if there is just one thing you should remember, it's this: there
are *too many* convergences to be an accident.

During my research, staggered by these extensive convergences, I asked perhaps the most urgent question of all.

Is there any correspondence between ancient traditions of the East and West? India and Israel? Yogis and Israelites?

Are they connected?

The answer blew me away. I think it will floor you, too.

EAST AND WEST CONVERGE

Section 5

GENESIS AND THE COSMIC EGG

YOU HAVE SEEN ONE HUNDRED MAJOR CONVERGENCES of ancient Yoga Literature and modern science.[147]

The proclamation of spirituality's ancient teachers that God exists is demonstrated by these correspondences. Surely, the vast number cannot be a coincidence. These ancients knew far more about our universe than could be expected of mere mortals.

In this section you will see twenty-one equally important correspondences from another ancient heritage: the Bible. Remarkably, its narrative of creation parallels that opined by the Yogis. Indeed, the sequence of creation in the Bible has close correspondences with the cosmic egg, or *brahmanda*. The terminology, of-course, is different. But the concepts are very similar.

Consider this: Firstly, without doubt, the description of creation given by the Yogis matches science closely. Secondly, the Biblical account corresponds with the Yogic account. Implication: The Bible converges with science, too. This wasn't realized earlier because Genesis is so brief and was thought to describe the creation of planet Earth.

How mistaken was this assumption!

It actually describes the formation of our ancient Milky Way Galaxy, a universe in itself.

As you have already seen, one of the reasons the correspondences of modern science with ancient yoga weren't fathomed earlier is because of the misinterpretation of three Sanskrit words: *brahmanda* ('cosmic egg'), *prithivi* ('earth'), and *padma* ('lotus'). Like your shirt buttons, if you fasten the first one wrong, all are fastened wrong. Similarly, translators misunderstood the basic word *brahmanda*. They translated it as 'universe.' So all went wrong.

Could it be, then, that the ancient Hebrew term for earth (*erets*) used in the very first line of the Bible has a similar cosmic context as *prithivi?* Could Genesis be describing the creation of our Milky Way Galaxy?

When we examine the passages closely, the answer is affirmative. An important clue to this fact is that all the words in Genesis[148] are used as abstractions. They are generalizations of real, tangible objects. Since the word 'earth' is cosmic, so are the other terms like heavens, water, abyss, and light. They are cosmic abstractions.

Here is the evidence.

Have you noticed in Genesis the absence of simple nouns like 'Sun' and 'Moon'? Instead, the passage uses *abstract* terms – 'lights in the expanse of the sky,' 'the greater light to rule the day,' and 'the lesser light to rule the night.'

God said, "Let there be lights in the expanse of sky to divide the day from the night ... .

God made the two great lights: the greater light to rule the day,
and the lesser light to rule the night.

Bible, Genesis 1:14-16

Why doesn't the passage simply use 'Sun' and 'Moon'? Common nouns for Sun and Moon, such as *shemesh* and *yareach* respectively, existed in Hebrew and were used every day by everyone. They are used frequently later in Genesis, too.[149]

So why not here in its very first section?

Simple: The first passages of Genesis are *intended* to be abstractions. The abstract theme continues throughout the narrative of creation. This includes the appearance of life on Earth. Instead of using specific nouns such as goat, sheep and cows, Genesis uses "cattle" or "grazing animals." Instead of bears, lions, and leopards, Genesis uses "wild animals." The entire theme is clearly an abstract description of creation. It's a beautiful and consistent rendition.

The challenge is here: How do you relate this abstraction to the real world? How can you deduce what it's actually referring to on each 'day'? Do you need to become a Biblical scholar or rocket scientist?

Far from them. Sometimes, when people are trapped inside the box of their profession, scholastics can actually make them one-eyed. They can develop 'tunnel vision' and miss the larger perspective. Too close to the pedantic details of their own work, they can't see the wood for the trees, so to speak. They become bound by unquestioned assumptions and entangled in the rules of their trade. Subduing these to burst out from their cage and cross forbidden borders becomes unthinkable to them.

Fortunately, today, the Bible is open for everyone to understand. To grasp Genesis, what is required isn't scholarship, but just a little knowledge of both Genesis and recently discovered cosmology. Then you just connect the dots.

Let's go back to the example of the Sun and Moon in Genesis on Day 4. Imagine this. If you were around before the Sun and Moon were created and read the above passage, you would wonder what those 'greater and lesser lights' may be. Then, one day, the Sun and Moon begin to form in the sky and you connect them to what you read in the Bible. Similarly, once you know a little more about our Galaxy, you will easily connect it to Genesis. Importantly, you will find that it all fits together coherently. Genesis suddenly makes a lot of sense. Its descriptions correspond to modern cosmology, geology, and biology.

Is this a fluke? Hardly. The chronological timeline converges too, right from the beginning of creation (the Big Bang) till the present – the appearance of human beings.

How is this? How can the 6-day calendar be compatible with science's chronicle of billions of years?

The issue has resounded for centuries. God created everything from heavens to humankind in 6 days, says Genesis. The universe to humankind was created in 13.7 billion years, say scientists. Who is right?

Both are right.

The dispute has arisen due to two shortcomings. 1) The faithful were unable to propose a coherent interpretation of the Biblical 6 days. Some suggested each day must be longer than 24 hours, but nobody was able to say how much longer. 2) Scientists were unclear about the age of the universe. Various theories proposed 10, 12, or 20 billion years.

Fortunately, in 2003, data from space-based telescopes helped resolve the issue and scientists declared the universe is 13.7 billion years old. Now, with this more precise figure, it's easy to see how long each Biblical day should be and how it converges with modern science. And it does so to an extraordinary degree.

Take a look at the following passage. Genesis describes the period of creation from start to finish as taking '6 days.' God rested on the seventh. (Words in parentheses are my insertions. Non-English words are Hebrew.)

The heavens (*shamayim*) and the earth (*erets*) were finished,
and all their vast array.
On the seventh day God finished his work which he had made;
and he rested on the seventh day
from all his work which he had made.

Bible, Genesis 2:1-2

It's easy to see that if the age of the universe is really 13.7 billion years old and if a Deity truly created it in 6 'days,' then each day should have a length of 13.7 billion / 6 =

2.283 billion years.[150]

Does this period make sense in terms of modern science? Is it truly the length of each day in Genesis? Can it be tested?

Yes! Here is the stunning proof and a preview of what is to come in following pages.

Science says our Sun and Moon formed 4.6 and 4.5 billion years ago, respectively. That means they have an average age of 4.55 billion years. Genesis states the Sun and Moon appeared on Day 4. How long ago would that be?

13.7 billion years − (2.283 billion years x 4 days) =

4.568 billion years ago.

It's exactly the same as modern science!

This is a stupendous correspondence. It can only occur if the universe is taken to be 13.7 billion years old. Any significantly different age would make Genesis beget the wrong age of our Sun. Its yielding the correct age is therefore statistically impossible to be a coincidence. Genesis *is vindicated*.

And there are more correspondences. Many, many more. With the new perspective, Genesis suddenly exhibits 21 major correspondences with our Galaxy.

Before we go to them, you may be interested in hearing a little about how I came upon this remarkable discovery.

In 2007, I finished the initial manuscript of this book. It contained many of the convergences of science and spirituality you have already seen from the Yoga Literature. It also had a few from the Bible, for instance our spherical Earth hanging in space. However, I had gotten a strong spiritual intuition that something major was missing. I narrated this dissonance to my wife. What could it be? We hadn't a clue and we ruled out Genesis completely. It didn't make any sense at all. Remember, I had personally concluded in my mind nearly two decades earlier, after His Holiness inspired me to study science and spirituality, that Genesis would forever remain beyond the realm of human comprehension.

Later, as I was waiting at our dining table for dinner, I prayed and meditated. I remained quiet with my eyes shut for several minutes and then, in a miraculous flash, arrived the answer!

It wasn't a single word or number but a whole concept and calculation. And it wasn't a hunch. I *knew* it was correct even though I hadn't processed the calculation and I'm not a mathematician who can do it in my head.

This is what came to me energetically and miraculously in that fraction of a moment: 'Genesis is not a description of our universe or Earth. It is a description of our Milky Way Galaxy. If you divide the age of the universe, which is 13.7 billion years, by the number of days of creation in Genesis, which is 6, the age of the Sun on Day 4 is 4.6 billion years – *without doubt*. The other 5 Days will also converge with our Galaxy.' I leapt out of my seat, grabbed a calculator (for formality's sake), and did the above calculation. The age of the Sun on Day 4 was indeed 4.6 billion years. My wife and I were flabbergasted. I then compared the rest of Genesis to the formation of our Galaxy.

What surfaced is amazing.

A DAY 2.283 BILLION YEARS LONG!

AN EON. THAT'S THE LENGTH OF THIS DAY! What about its description? As you've seen, the account of creation described in Genesis is an abstraction. It's therefore reasonable that a comparison with our Galaxy should be abstract and generalized, too. In this section, you'll see how this comparison makes sense and how its new timeline corresponds with modern science. Following are relevant excerpts.

DAY 1

In the beginning God created the heavens and the earth.
Now the earth was formless and empty.
Darkness was on the surface of the deep.
God's Spirit was hovering over the surface of the waters.
God said, "Let there be light," and there was light.
God saw the light, and saw that it was good.

God divided the light from the darkness.
God called the light "day," and the darkness he called "night."
There was evening and there was morning, one day.

Bible, Genesis 1:1-5

Right at the outset, before we cover anything else, I want to draw your attention to something tremendously important that is often missed in this first passage. It mentions the words 'day,' 'morning,' and 'evening.' Have you noticed there is no mention of the Sun and Moon? That's because they aren't created until Day 4. That means the 'day,' 'morning,' and 'evening' spoken of on Day 1 cannot refer to our 24 hour solar day. The 24 hour day is created on Day 4 when God creates the Sun and Moon and actually *says*, 'let them be for signs, and for seasons, and *for days* and years.' The day spoken of on Day 1 of Genesis is different. It is a day of the Lord himself. It's an *eon*. More amazing evidence on this later.

For now, let us move on to the correspondences.

The first words of Genesis say, "In the beginning God created the heavens and earth." This statement is like a heading, an introduction. This is clear because Genesis itself shows that the heavens and earth are not completed until Days 2 and 3. It took 2-3 Days to create heaven and earth.

However, a formless and empty 'earth' had already appeared on Day 1. Genesis starts with a description of its condition at that time. The narrator simply says "the earth was formless and empty ... darkness was on the surface of the deep ... God's Spirit was hovering over the surface of the waters ... God said, "Let there be light," and there was light." This is the core message of the passage.

Let us now consider all these elements. What are the 'earth,' 'waters,' and 'light' that appear in this order, on Day 1? (Remarkably, the heavens are created on Day 2, after the earth, just like in the Yoga Literature.[151])

What does the word 'earth' refer to? Does it refer to our spherical planet Earth as commonly assumed? To me, as we have seen in accordance with Genesis's cosmic theme, the term 'earth' must be in reference to something abstract and generalized. What could that be? It refers to the *element* earth. Simple *dust*. It's the dust that filled our early Galaxy. Remember, there was enough to obscure its resplendent stars.

There is much evidence to support this view. Four Biblical passages converge with modern science.

Convergence 1

This concerns the description of earth on Day 1. It is 'formless and empty.'

How can our solid, spherical (or even 'flat' for that matter) Earth be described as formless, without shape? It cannot. But the passage does relate closely to our early Galaxy filled with dust which is easier to imagine as formless and empty.

Convergence 2

This concerns the presence of water within that early formation.

What does this water refer to? It cannot refer to oceans on 'earth' because it was formless and empty. The water referred to here is again elemental. It speaks of the *element* water. The passage relates to the water created by stars spread across our early Galaxy.

Here, there is another eye-opening convergence connecting Genesis to ancient Yoga Literature. Just as Day 1 of Genesis states that God's Spirit presided or hovered over those primordial waters, so too does the Yoga Literature. In their own terminology, the Yogis used the word Purusha and Narayana for God.

Purusha [Narayana] ... created pure water ...
he resided on that water [for an eon].

Bhagavata Purana 2.10.10-11

Remember, the Yogis described these waters as belonging to the cosmic egg, not our planet Earth. It was cosmic, elemental water. Not the water of our oceans.

Convergence 3

This concerns the absence of light. The formless earth and waters were shrouded in darkness. That was exactly the initial condition of our Galaxy: dusty, watery, and dark.[152] The light of its stars, though luminous, was shrouded by dust.

Convergence 4

This concerns the appearance of light. What was its source?

It wasn't the Sun because it was created on Day 4. Some have claimed it refers to the electromagnetic energy of the Big Bang.

But this is untenable because Genesis states that the light appeared towards the *end* of the first day, not at its beginning. The formless and empty earth was there before it.

The light of Genesis was more likely that of the blazing halo stars and bulge of our Galaxy. This cosmic structure became an enduring source of resplendent light as the dust cleared. It was the luminous cosmic egg of the Yogis.

What about the timeline? Does it correlate, too?

Convergence 5

You have seen that if both scientific discovery and Biblical revelation are true, then one 'Day of the Lord' should equal 2.283 billion years.

The emergence of 'permanent' light in our Galaxy debuted with the formation of its halo and central bulge between 13-10 billion years ago. Since the period of one day in Genesis is 2.283 billion years, would this permanent light have appeared within this period? Indeed.

13.7 billion years − (2.283 billion years x 1 day) =

11.42 billion years ago.

This is a remarkable correlation with the appearance of our Galaxy's halo and bulge 13-10 billion years ago. Moreover, the ancient Yogis said the same thing. Primordial light did not come from our Sun which was created much later. First light came from the luminescent cosmic egg which was made up of stars!

DAY 2

God said, "Let there be an expanse (or atmosphere, *raqiya*)
in the middle of the waters,
and let it divide the waters from the waters." ... and it was so.
God called the expanse (or atmosphere, *raqiya*) "sky"
(or heavens, *shamayim*).
There was evening and there was morning, a second day.

Bible, Genesis 1:6-8

Convergence 6

Day 2 is when the sky or heavens (*shamayim*) is created. First, God divided the masses of cosmic water by inserting within it a central 'expanse.'

What might this refer to? We know that science has discovered there was an abundance of water produced by stars igniting all over the early Galaxy. We also know that our watery Galaxy was 'divided' into two at its center by the settling of a vast disk of gas. (Figure 3.3)

Could this gaseous disk be the cosmic expanse referred to in Genesis?

Consider this: The Hebrew word for expanse is *raqiya*. It means 'expanse, sky, vault, firmament, or atmosphere.'[153] From these meanings it is clear that *raqiya* refers to some sort of *gase-*

ous formation – just like the early disk of gas 'dividing' our Milky Way at its center.

Does the timeline correlate, too?

Convergence 7

Science says the gaseous disk evolved between 10-8 billion years ago.[154]

Genesis states the completion of the gaseous expanse (*raqiya*) marked the end of Day 2. This adds 2.283 billion years to its time-line.

13.7 billion years – (2.283 billion years x 2 days) =

9.134 billion years ago.

This corresponds with the formation of the gaseous disk dividing our Galaxy between 10-8 billion years ago.

DAY 3

God said, "Let the waters under the sky (or heavens,
shamayim) be gathered together to one place,
and let the dry land appear";
and it was so.
God called the dry land "earth,"
and the gathering together of the waters he called "seas."

God saw that it was good.
God said, "Let the earth yield grass, herbs yielding seed,
and fruit trees ... and it was so ... and God saw that it was good.
There was evening and there was morning, a third day.

Bible, Genesis 1:9-13

Convergence 8

This concerns the appearance of dry land and vegetation on Day 3.

What is this dry land (*erets*)? Does it refer to planet Earth? Close, but not exactly. More generally, it refers to the first habitable worlds: Earth-like planets within the gaseous expanse (*raqiya*).

Remember, the context of Genesis is cosmic. These planets provided the first 'dry land.' It is where vegetation would have appeared. And science indeed predicts that if conditions are favorable, plant and other life would have evolved on these planets. It is impossible that the author of Genesis believed all these seeds, plants, and fruit trees would flourish and bloom in utter darkness on our planet when there was still no Sun or Moon. Remember, ancient people were as rational as we are. No one knew better than they that harvests depended on the Sun and seasons. Yet, according to the author of Genesis, the Sun and Moon were still to be created. They appear on Day 4.

Let's analyze the timeline of Day 3.

Convergence 9

Science says Earth-like planets developed in our Galaxy's gaseous disk between 7-5 billion years ago. Genesis says 'dry land' appeared towards the completion of Day 3. Does it correlate?

13.7 billion years – (2.283 billion years x 3 days) =

6.85 billion years ago.

This is a remarkable convergence with science's estimate of 7-5 billion years ago. And there is yet another correlation with the ancient Yogis. They said that the 'earthy world' refers to wherever as far as the stars there is land that can be walked on.[155] Land doesn't refer only to planet Earth.

DAY 4

God said, "Let there be lights in the expanse of sky
to divide the day from the night;
and let them be for signs, and for seasons,
and for days and years;
and let them be for lights in the expanse (*raqiya*) of sky
(*shamayim*) to give light on the earth"; and it was so.
God made the two great lights: the greater light to rule the day,
and the lesser light to rule the night. He also made the stars. ...
God saw that it was good.
There was evening and there was morning, a fourth day.

A DAY 2.283 BILLION YEARS LONG!

Bible, Genesis 1:14-19

Convergence 10

Day 4 concerns the appearance of two lights in the sky.

You saw earlier that it's clear they refer to our Sun and Moon. It's remarkable that Genesis states that the Sun, Moon, and stars were created *within* the gaseous cosmic expanse. This indeed is where our Sun, Moon, and all the night stars are located according to science. They are within our Galaxy's gaseous disk.

But what about the timeline?

Convergence 11

Science pins down the appearance of our Sun accurately to 4.6 billion years ago and the appearance of our Moon to about 4.5 billion years ago.

Does Genesis correspond? We saw earlier:

13.7 billion years – (2.283 billion years x 4 days) =

4.568 billion years ago.

This is a tremendous correlation with modern science!

How can all the above 11 correspondences occur by accident?

Convergence 12

This concerns the appearance of the night stars. Day 4 states that after the Sun and Moon, God created the stars. These are, of-course, the objects we see overhead with the naked eye, like the Sun and Moon. Indeed, at the age of 4.6 billion years, our Sun is a relatively mature star amongst the stars around it. The majority of stars we see in the night sky were born *after* our Sun and are younger to it by 1 to 4 billion years.[156]

How could the narrator of Genesis know this?

DAY 5

God said, "Let the waters swarm with swarms
of living creatures, and let birds fly above the earth
in the open expanse of sky."
God created the large sea creatures,
and every living creature that moves,
with which the waters swarmed, after their kind,
and every winged bird after its kind.
God saw that it was good ... .
There was evening and there was morning, a fifth day.

Bible, Genesis 1:20-23

Day 5 concerns the appearance of life on our planet. After refer-ring to the Sun, Moon, and night stars on Day 4, Genesis's description becomes local, focusing on planet Earth from Day 5 onwards. Nevertheless, it remains abstract and generalized. Day 5 states that life on our planet first appeared in the oceans. Birds are also mentioned.

Convergence 13

Science agrees. Life first appeared in the oceans and then on land. It began with microbes and simple multicellular life. Eventually, the oceans swarmed with complex and large creatures.

What about the timeframe?

Convergence 14

According to science, animal life from microbes to simple multicellular life appeared in the oceans from 3.5-1 billion years ago. This is an average of 2.25 billion years ago.

According to Genesis, the timeframe window for the appearance of life in the oceans is

13.7 billion years – (2.283 billion years x 5 days) =

2.285 billion years ago

This is yet another remarkable correlation with science.

But there is something else of great importance in the passage describing Day 5. The narrator does not state the usual, "and it was so." Why? Simple. Because it was not yet completely *so*. God had initiated the process of putting life forms on Earth, but it would not truly culminate until Day 6 when the narrator *does* say, "and it was so." So what was it that was not completed on Day 5? The appearance of complex and large oceanic animals, and later, birds. They appear on Day 6 when the narrator affirms the actualization of

God's wishes described in Days 5 *and* 6 by saying, "and it was so." The narrator's omission of this phrase in Day 5, thereby correctly describing the appearance of complex and large oceanic animals, and later, birds on Day 6, was a stroke of genius!

DAY 6

God said, "Let the earth produce living creatures
after their kind, livestock, creeping things,
and animals of the earth after their kind"; and it was so ... .
God made the animals of the earth after their kind, and the
livestock after their kind, and everything that creeps on the
ground after its kind. God saw that it was good.
God said, "Let us make man in our image, after our likeness ... .
... and it was so ... . God saw everything that he had made,
and, behold, it was very good.
There was evening and there was morning, a sixth day.

Bible, Genesis 1:24-31

Convergence 15-18

According to science, a rich crowd of animals appeared in the oceans between 545-490 million years ago. Between 417-354 million years ago, numerous types of fish appeared. Birds appeared about 150 million years ago. Then, much later, about 60 million years ago hunting, carnivorous cats and dogs appeared. Early horses and elephants also appeared. About 55 million years ago, early ancestors of pigs, sheep, and cows appeared. Early relatives of humans, like the tool-making *Homo habilis*, the 'handy man' arrived considerably later about 2.5-2 million years ago.

Genesis describes a similar chronology!

15. Complex and large animals appeared in the oceans.
16. Then birds.
17. Then cattle and other animals.
18. Lastly, humankind.

The timeframe given by science is 545-2 million years ago. What is the window given by Genesis?

Convergence 19

According to Genesis:

13.7 billion years – (2.283 billion years x 6 days) =

between 2.283 billion to 2 million years ago.

This is another remarkable correspondence. The appearance of all the life forms described in Genesis fall well within the window described by science.

Indeed, the whole of Genesis converges magnificently with the creation of our Milky Way Galaxy and life on planet Earth!

There are still *two more* convergences, however. They emerge from descriptions elsewhere in the Bible of Day 7. These future events correctly correspond to scientific facts concerning the future condition of our Earth. (See *End of the Age*, p. 191.) In total, then, there are twenty-one staggering correspondences!

CONVERGENCES ACROSS THE BOARD

IT IS DIFFICULT TO CONCLUDE THAT the numerous and major convergences you have seen are just an accident. How can they be regarded as a *second* fluke assembly of a launch-ready space shuttle, the other being by the ancient Yogis? Individually, neither tradition's convergences can be flukes, both together even less so.

It is clear that right from the beginning of Genesis – from the description of the watery abyss, the appearance of light, the formation of the gaseous divider through to the appearance of the Sun, Moon, stars, animal life in our oceans and then on land, and finally the appearance of human beings – all this comprises a beautiful abstraction of the cosmic drama of our Galaxy's creation. Each stage of creation superimposes splendidly with modern science descriptively, sequentially, and chronologically.[157] You can compare them easily in Table 1. Statistically, it is impossible to be an accident. Significantly, at each step, too, there are convergences with ancient Yoga Literature which you saw also echo science to an extraordinary degree.

21 out of 21 descriptions correct = 100 percent.

SCIENCE	*The Big Bang*	GENESIS	
13.7 Billion Years Ago	2.283 Billion Years	Beginning of 1st Day	
Cosmic Dust, Cosmic Water, Light of Stellar Halo & Bulge. **11.4 Billion Years Ago**		Earth, Water, Light. End of 1st Day	**DAY** **1**
Galaxy's Gaseous Disk, Water Divided Above and Below It. **9.1 Billion Years Ago**	2.283 Billion Years	Gaseous Expanse, Water Divided Above and Below It. End of 2nd Day	**DAY** **2**
Galaxy's Earth-Like Planets, Vegetation. **6.8 Billion Years Ago**	2.283 Billion Years	Land, Vegetation. End of 3rd Day	**DAY** **3**
Our Sun, Moon, Night Stars. **4.6 Billion Years Ago**	2.283 Billion Years	Sun, Moon, Night Stars. End of 4th Day	**DAY** **4**
On Earth - Microbial Animal Life & Simple Multicellular Life in Oceans. **2.3 Billion Years Ago**	2.283 Billion Years	Beginnings of Animal Life in Oceans. End of 5th Day	**DAY** **5**
Complex & Large Animal Life in Oceans, Birds, Cattle & Other Animals, Human Beings. **2 Million Years Ago**	2.283 Billion Years	Complex & Large Animal Life in Oceans, Birds, Cattle & Other Animals, Human Beings. End of 6th Day	**DAY** **6**
CURRENT ERA **FUTURE ERA** Volcanic Fire, Brimstone. End of Life on Earth After 1-2 Billion Years. **2.283 Billion Years in Future**	2.283 Billion Years	CURRENT ERA **FUTURE ERA** Volcanic Fire, Brimstone. End of Life on Earth *End of the Age* or *The End of Days.* End of 7th Day	**DAY** **7**

Table 1. When the scientific timeline of 13.7 billion years is calibrated into 6 equal days – each spanning 2.283 billion years – the sequence of each phase in Genesis and its timeline across all 7 Days corresponds with major past and future episodes of our Galaxy and Earth. (For details of Day 7 see *End of the Age*, p. 191.) In total, there are 21 correspondences.

Genesis is no doubt a legitimate, 3,000 years old abstraction of a cosmology discovered by science only within the last few decades.[158] (Figure 5.1)

Nevertheless, as I stated earlier with regard to the Yoga Literature, it doesn't serve to tell incomplete truths. Not all is perfect, and neither can it be expected. Genesis is an abstraction, a generalization. Moreover, it's brief, symbolic, and cryptic.

As such, there remains a small enigma. This concerns the appearance of 'creeping things' or insects on Day 6. Their appearance during Day 6 is correct, when the narrator says, "and it was so." But their appearance after cattle seems odd. They should have appeared first. And, to me, it's apparent they did. Genesis states that complex and large creatures appeared first (in the oceans). It is clear that this chronology overlaps with the appearance of complex and large creatures on Day 6 on land when God says, "and it was so" on behalf of *both* Days 5 and 6.

This superb accuracy of Genesis is further supported by its correct prediction of what will happen on Earth towards the end of Day 7, in around a couple of billion years. The Bible states that all life on Earth will come to an end. There will be volcanic fire. Science agrees. This means all 21 out of 21 descriptions and timelines in Genesis are correct!

PERHAPS, ONE OF THE MOST IMPORTANT facts to emerge from our study of Genesis is that a creation day is different from a solar day.

The solar day was created on Day 4 for the purpose of seasons, *days,* and years. This description of Day 4 makes it clear that the days spoken of earlier were of a different character.

Indeed, the ancient Israelites (and Yogis) taught that we experience time differently from the way God does. His 'day' is much longer. It's an eon. This is evident from Day 4 in Genesis as well as the correspondences with science you have just seen. It's also implicit in Psalm and 2 Peter. In the following hymn of praise traditionally believed written by Moses, we hear:

For a thousand years
in your sight
are just like yesterday when it is past,
like a watch in the night.

Bible, Psalm 90:4

Similarly, Peter, one of the great leaders of early Christianity, says:

But don't forget this one thing, beloved,
that one day is with the Lord
as a thousand years,
and a thousand years as one day.

Bible, 2 Peter 3:8

Fig 5.1. Genesis: an abstract and cryptic description of the creation of our Milky Way Galaxy. (Artist's impression.)

Till now, naysayers have tried to prove there is no God on the basis of an apparent conflict between science and ancient spirituality, in particular, Biblical Genesis. But their opinion can no longer be upheld. To do so would be to entirely ignore these huge correspondences and their implications.

Today, it doesn't require complex studies to notice the extensive convergence of Genesis with our Milky Way Galaxy. All that is required is familiarity with basic facts about the two.

In today's scientific era, the Bible and Yoga Literature have emerged as ancient masterpieces open for all to understand and admire.

END OF THE AGE

HOW COULD THE INSPIRERS of these ancient scriptures know so much about our universe and Galaxy? How could they achieve this without using modern instruments? It is evident they must have had access to a deeper wisdom that revealed all these truths to them. The gateway to this knowledge was the practice of Faith, Prayer, and the universal principles of Yoga.

Israelites had their own tradition of yoga. This is discernible from the following statements in the Bible. "Be still, and know that I am God." (Psalm 46:10) "I have stilled and quieted my soul." (Psalm 131:2) "Of the glorious majesty of thine honor, And of thy wondrous works, will I meditate." (Psalm 145:5) "I will meditate on thy precepts, And have respect unto thy ways." (Psalm 119:15) Jesus said, "Therefore don't be anxious, saying, 'What will we eat?', 'What will we drink?' or, 'With what will we be clothed?' ... But seek first God's Kingdom ... ." (Matthew 6:31-34) He taught people to seek this kingdom of God within: "The Kingdom of God doesn't come with observation; neither will they say, 'Look, here!' or, 'Look, there!' for behold, the Kingdom of God is within you." (Luke 17:21) These are the *very same* principles as

191

those of Yogic meditation: it advises you should live in the present moment and seek God within your soul.

Many people ask me, "Is meditating on God and meditating on his precepts the same thing?" The answer is *yes*, because those precepts are all connected to God. They are holy. Therefore they are worthy of meditation.

These, then, are the principles of Yoga. Practicing them with faith and stillness of mind would, for some, lead to the rare knowledge of the universe revealed in Genesis. For everyone, however, it will bring something vastly more important: peace to the soul.

Back to the world. Remember the section on superclusters of galaxies? You saw the celebrated motif of the Nataraja depicting the dance of innumerable cosmic eggs and the belief that our Earth will end in fire.

What kind of fire did the Yogis say it would be? Forest fire? Volcanic fire? Warfare fire? Nope.

Solar fire.

The end of our planet will be dealt by the Sun. They said 'the end' will begin in 2.35 billion years due to heat from the Sun and volcanism, the Aurvanala you met in Sections 1 and 2. There will be no life on Earth, its surface will be scorched and barren, and there will be no oceans. Eventually, the Sun will swell a hundredfold, engulf the Earth and melt it.

The Yogis also said this period of destruction by the Sun will end after a further 4.32 billion years. This means about 6.7 billion years in the future.[159] But is all this true? *Yes!*

Our Sun is slowly expanding, says science. In about 2 billion years time, our Earth will be so hot there will be no life on it.[160] Its surface will be scorched and barren, and there will be no oceans. Instead, the land will flow with lava. Volcanism will be common on the planet's surface. Earth will be a living hell, its surface scorched by the fire of lava and sulfur (brimstone) from exploding volcanoes.[161] Eventually, the Sun's heat will melt the Earth. In about 7.6 billion years from now, the Sun will probably engulf and vaporize it.[162] By this time our Sun will have grown to about 149-179 times its current radius.[163] After puffing out its outer shells it will live on as a small, faint white dwarf star.

The convergence of the Yoga Literature with this prediction is incredible. Elegantly, it leads us to yet another connection with the Bible.

Convergence 20

For, behold, the day comes, it burns as a furnace.

Bible, Malachi 4:1

But the heavens that now are, and the earth, by the same word
have been stored up for fire ... .
But the day of the Lord will come as a thief in the night;
in which the heavens will pass away with a great noise,
and the elements will be dissolved with fervent heat,
and the earth and the works that are in it will be burned up. ...
the coming of the day of God,
which will cause the burning heavens to be dissolved ... .

Bible, 2 Peter 3:10-12

Behold, I am with you always, even to the end of the age.

Bible, Matthew 28:20, 24:3

The devil who deceived them [will be] thrown
into the lake of fire and sulfur ... .[164]

Bible, Revelation 20:10

Again, the Bible converges with science! The final days of our Earth will be of blazing conflagration. The planet's surface will be melted. By mentioning the "lake of fire and sulfur," the Bible makes it clear that the source of fire is volcanism. All life on Earth will end. However, the Yoga Literature clarifies that *that* signifies only the beginning of the end. Earth's final death blow will be dealt by the Sun. It will swell a hundred-fold, engulf our Earth, and heat it into a molten ball. The Yogis' timeline converges with science, too.

Does the Biblical timeline also converge? According to Genesis, we have just begun Day 7. The glaring question is: What will happen at its culmination? Above, 2 Peter and other passages describe it as the "Day of God" and say it will inaugurate the "End of the Age," the destruction of our Earth by volcanic fire.

We can work out when in the future this will be.

Convergence 21

Since we have already begun Day 7, its end through volcanism, or the End of the Age, will arrive in about 2.28 billion years. Remarkably, this is similar to the timeframe given by science of about 2 billion years. It also coincides with 2.35 billion years given by the Yogis for the commencement of Earth's destruction by volcanism and its total annihilation later by the Sun after 6.7 billion years.

We have clear evidence, here, that the mention in the Bible of the End of the Age or the Day of God when some creatures are seared by lakes of burning sulfur is not nonsense. It is a metaphor depicting violent volcanic activity in eras to come.

IN ALL, YOU HAVE SEEN NINETEEN MAJOR numerical convergences like these between the Bible, ancient Yoga Literature, and modern science. The vast majority hit the bull's-eye. The remaining come very close to it. All of the convergences are remarkable considering the infinite choice of *wrong* timelines the ancients could have proposed if they did it through sheer fantasy. Equally accurate are the descriptions of biological, geological, and cosmic events associated with these timelines. All the descriptions cohere and tally with science. See Tables 2 and 3 below for a summary.

	Scientific Figures (predicted)	Yogic Figures (explicit)
1	Volcanic fire scorched India about 118 million years ago. It emerged in the southern Indian Ocean soon after about 112 million years ago. It emerged *above* the ocean about 100 million years ago.	120.9-118.8 million years ago

	Scientific Figures (predicted)	Yogic Figures (explicit)
2-4	It was a vicious 'fish eat fish' world between 417-354 million years ago. Life on Earth faced global extinction between 251-200 million years ago. Oceans flooded large parts of many continents worldwide between between 240-200 million years ago and 175-112 million years ago.	429-120.5 million years ago
5	Today, there are about 8.7 million species of life.	8.4 million species
6	Elementary particles of gas formed within a second after the Big Bang.	0.64 seconds
7	The Galaxy's halo and bulge developed 13-10 billion years ago.	14.9-10.6 billion years ago
8	Its disk with inhabitable worlds evolved 7-5 billion years ago.	6.3 billion years ago
9	The Galaxy will shine for another 100 trillion years.	155 trillion years
10	Earth will be a hell of fire and sulfur in about 2 billion years.	2.35 billion years
11	The future Sun will expand 149-179 times its radius.	100 times
12	The expanded Sun will melt the Earth in about 7.6 billion years.	6.7 billion years

Table 2: Twelve major numerical convergences between science and ancient Yoga Literature.

	Scientific Figures (predicted)	Biblical Figures (implicit)
1	The Galaxy's halo and bulge developed 13-10 billion years ago.	11.42 billion years ago
2	The Galaxy's gaseous disk evolved between 10-8 billion years ago	9.134 billion years ago
3	Earth-like planets developed in our Galaxy's gaseous disk between 7-5 billion years ago	6.85 billion years ago
4	Appearance of Sun and Moon 4.6-4.5 billion years ago.	4.568 billion years ago.
5	Appearance of microbial animal life and simple multi-cellular life in oceans 3.5-1 billion years ago.	2.285 billion years ago
6	Appearance of early relatives of humans 2.5-2 million years ago.	2 million years ago
7	End of life on Earth. It will be a hell of volcanic fire and sulfur in about 2 billion years.	2.28 billion years

Table 3: Seven major numerical convergences between science and the Bible.

In Tables 2 and 3 above, there are 12 Yogic + 7 Biblical = 19 major numerical convergences. They are superb. They are all the more remarkable because the Yogic and Biblical timelines converge *with each other.*

Nevertheless, all this is only the tip of the iceberg.

THREE AND FOURTEEN REALMS

ANCIENT YOGIS AND ISRAELITES DESCRIBED some amazing spiritual experiences. For instance, they said that the cosmic egg consists of three and fourteen 'worlds' or realms.

Though this topic in the ancient literature doesn't really refer to our physical world, but primarily to a mystical realm, I'm delving into this discussion of the three and fourteen realms because this book is also about major convergences between ancient spiritual traditions.

Amongst these, a very important convergence is that both Eastern *and* Western traditions opined this belief in three and fourteen realms! That these realms do not relate to the physical sciences does not to me diminish the importance of this convergence. Here's why.

Firstly, the convergence implies that the differences between the two traditions are quite minimal beneath the surface, even from a spiritual perspective.

Secondly, and even more importantly, they imply the mystical realms are not fictitious. The Israelites and Yogis didn't make it all up as they went along any more than they did the colossal scientific convergences you have witnessed in both traditions. Their references to three and fourteen realms weren't fantasy. They were a cryptic message filled with exuberance. They were about a mystical, spiritual experience. And it was a universal one.

As one celebrated Yogi explained:

I have experienced this myself ... .
As one meditates, one sees the Lord's cosmic form
and within it the Fourteen Realms.

As one meditates in this way,
all the objects described in scripture come to view.
Consequently, any remaining doubts [as of their existence]
are dissolved and the soul
becomes exceedingly strong and emboldened.

Vachanamruta, Amdavad 1; Mahabharata, 12.188

As you can see from the quote above, the descriptions of three and fourteen realms came from spiritual people who had seen something real, but beyond our daily experience.

Let us take a closer look at these realms.

IN THE EARLIEST OF YOGA LITERATURE, the Rig Veda, there are two mystical hymns regarding the creation of our cosmic egg. One hymn is the *Nasadiya Sukta.* (We will see this shortly.) The second is the *Purusha Sukta.* This describes the celebrated 'Purusha Sacrifice' or 'the Lord's Sacrifice.' The Purusha was the First Avatar or appearance of God in our locale of the universe.

The Avatar manifested as a cosmic structure. It comprised of the five physical elements and had enormous proportions. It was also complex with thousands of appendages. These are described metaphorically as 'arms,' 'legs,' 'eyes,' and 'heads.'[165] Thus, the earliest Yogis described this cosmic structure in terms of a cosmic man, a 'macranthropus' with thousands of limbs. He symbolically gives up his body in a sacrifice deliberated by divinities who reconstruct it into Three Realms, one above the other.

Purusha, who has a thousand heads, a thousand eyes,
a thousand feet ...

Purusha is verily all this (visible world) ... .

When the divinities performed the sacrifice
with Purusha as the offering ... .

With him the divinities ... and ... seers sacrificed ...

When they immolated Purusha,
into how many portions did they divide him? ... .

The Moon was born from his mind;
the Sun was born from his eye ... .

THREE AND FOURTEEN REALMS

From his navel came the firmament,
from his head the heaven was produced,
the earth from his feet ... .

So they constituted the (three-tiered[166]) realm (*loka*).

Rig Veda Samhita, Purusha Sukta, 10.90[167]

Later Yogis gave a detailed description of these Three Realms. They said it was in the shape of a disk. It's an enormous revolving wheel of gas, stars, and planets at the center of the *brahmanda*, the cosmic egg. The numerous correspondences you saw earlier show there is no doubt it is none other than the starry disk of our Milky Way Galaxy. Accordingly, the primordial multi-appendaged Purusha that preceded it can be none other than our proto-galaxy – its thousands of streams of stars fusing to form the cosmic egg and its central disk of stars. (Figures 3.3, 3.4, and 3.5)

The Purusha Sacrifice is a metaphorical testament to the grace of the Lord who, in the form of this multi-armed cosmic structure, offered himself up for the creation of the Three Realms. These regions would become the habitat of mortals engaged in the performance of action or 'karma.' It's also where they would reap its rewards. The Three Realms are famously referred to as *Bhuh-Bhuvah-Svah* or Earth-Firmament-Heaven by the later Yogis. The entire cosmic unit is sacred because it was born from the Lord's Avatar. All of it is holy.

A similar belief in Three Realms can be found in the Biblical tradition. Though not formally using the term Three Realms, the description of creation in Genesis does depict a three-tiered cosmic unit. It describes God as inserting the sky or 'heavens' (*shamayim,* plural) directly over the earth, thus relocating the waters below the earth and above the heavens.[168] Using the plural form, *shamayim,* implies at least two heavens above the earth. The first is obviously the 'sky' or 'firmament' and the second is heaven above it. This gives us Earth, Firmament, and Heaven. *Bhuh-Bhuvah-Svah.* The Three Realms of the Yogis.

More commonly found in the Bible, however, is the phrase 'heaven and earth.' It's simply an abbreviation for 'Earth, Firmament, and Heaven.' The firmament wasn't emphasized by ancient Israelites. It contains just the Sun and stars. Their beliefs centered around events on earth and God's rule from heaven. Look at it another way. If an executive speaks of her offices in London and New York, she will rarely mention the ocean in between. It isn't very relevant.

The same abbreviation, not surprisingly, was used by the earliest Yogis. Their mantras can be found in the Rig Veda. 'Heaven and Earth' is mentioned numerous times. However, like in Genesis, the tripartite cosmos is still clear. That the firmament in the middle isn't always mentioned by the earliest Yogis is because, to them, it wasn't as important as Heaven, which symbolized the 'Father,' and Earth the 'Mother.' *Dyava Prithivi* – 'Heaven and Earth' – was the beloved mantra of these earliest Yogis. It was the same for the ancient Israelites. It was an abbreviation. To them, the firmament was hardly worth mentioning. Their passion was for Heaven and Earth.

This leads us to the interesting question of why the slightly later Yogis thought the firmament *was* worth mentioning. Why was their mantra *Bhuh-Bhuvah-Svah?* Answer: for the same reason the early Yogis *didn't* mention it – personal preference, context, and emphasis.

Indeed, some of the later Yogis also described multiple heavens and earths. They revealed that there are actually *seven* 'heavens' and seven 'earths' comprising a total of fourteen realms. All of these realms can alternatively be grouped into three realms depending on how they're visualized.

Various Jewish and Christian texts also describe 1, 3, 5, and 7 heavens. There are also rare references to 8, 10, or 1,000 heavens. By and large, however 1 and 7 tiers were predominant.[169]

Some skeptics will no doubt try to show these variations as evidence of 'no God' or 'development of an idea' across hundreds of years. All this about heaven and earth is made up, they say.

The reality is, the variations exist purely due to the narrator emphasizing or abridging one point over another. Indeed, some Yogis eulogized both bipartite and tripartite realms within the *same* hymn.[170] The same practice is found within passages of early Jewish and Christian texts.[171] This clearly shows there was no development of the 'idea' from one to three or more tiers across hundreds of years. These multiple versions existed contemporaneously and were just various systems of representation, in various contexts. The number of tiers depended on how they were *grouped*. The later Yogis explained this themselves.

Breaking the egg there came forth from it
that very Purusha who has a thousand thighs,
feet, arms and eyes, a thousand mouths and heads,
from whose limbs the wise construct the realms:
seven downward and seven upward from the hip.

Alternatively, the construction of the realms
may be thus:
the earthy realm (*bhurloka*) was constructed from his feet,

the atmospheric **realm** (*bhuvarloka*) from his navel,
and the heavenly **realm** (*svarloka*) from his head.

Bhagavata Purana 2.5. 35-36, 42

Entering the bud of the lotus,
impelled by the action of the Lord,
he [Brahma] then split the one [lotus] in many ways,
dividing it into three [and] into twice seven.[172]

In this way was the division of the structure of the world
of living beings set up.

Bhagavata Purana 3.10.4-9

Whether 3 or 14 realms are referred to by the Yogis, then, is *not* a result of an incremental development of ideas. It was a result of mystical experience and context. Three or fourteen realms were enumerated depending on how they were grouped.

Most importantly, Yogis, Israelites, and many others around the world from widely differing traditions reported the same spiritual experience. Their beliefs converged.

What is so important about these realms?

SACRED COSMOLOGY

IN ANCIENT TIMES, COSMOLOGY WAS IMPORTANT. In fact, it was fundamental.[173] Teachers used it as a template to answer theological questions. If theology was the text, cosmology was the context. Once you understood the cosmology, the theology fell into place. That cosmology was central to the ancients is demonstrated by the fact that it's the *very first* topic in the Bible. It's also the first topic in the Yoga Literature, especially the *Puranas*. You can't get more prominent placements than that.

The reason for this pre-eminence was because the cosmos was sacred. It was holy. The entire cosmic world containing the heavens and earths that the Lord had built was his Temple. Within it, he would 'rest' or reside.

Thus says Yahweh, "Heaven is my throne,
and the earth is my footstool:

what kind of house will you build to me?
and what place shall be my rest?"

Bible, Isaiah 66:1

In all this [world, and in] all life
in this moving world, the Lord resides.

Isha Upanishad 1.1

Cosmology was therefore a holy science. The configuration of the cosmic structure God had built was of paramount importance. We have seen that ancient Yogis and Israelites opined it comprised seven heavens and seven earths.

Why did they describe the cosmic egg as configured this way? Was it numerology?

No. I must emphasize here that there was nothing intrinsically spiritual or special about the number seven. The number itself was not divine, transcendental, or perfect. It was just a number – just like any other. But it acquired holiness *through association.* Since, for whatever purposes, God completed the cosmos in this configuration (7+7) and duration (7 'Days'), Yogis and Israelites hallowed it. It became a *symbol* of completion. They therefore favored it to represent completion of other objects and events, too, whether or not they may have actually occurred in sevens.

There are many examples. Let us first consider the Bible. The number seven can be found couched in Genesis especially, and throughout the Bible in numerous ways.[174]

❖ The very first sentence of Genesis, in other words, the very first sentence of the Bible, in Hebrew, contains seven words. Moreover, they comprise 28 letters (7x4).[175] The second sentence contains 14 words (7x2). Even the number of times certain words occur in Genesis are in exact multiples of seven. The word 'God,' for instance, occurs 35 times (7x5), 'earth' 21 times (7x3), and 'heavens/firmament' 21 times (7x3). During the narrative, the phrase 'and it was so' occurs seven times and so, too, the phrase 'God saw that it was good.'[176] Finally, on Day 7, 'the seventh day' is mentioned in three sentences, each with seven words. This emphasized the sacredness of Day 7, the Sabbath, when God *completed* creation and rested.[177]

  None of this is by accident. The ancient authors utilized the multiple of seven to describe God's completed cosmos using this symbol.

❖ Noah is described as waiting seven days before again releasing a dove from the Ark to find dry land. It returned with an olive leaf and he waited another seven days before he released it again. (Genesis 8:10-12)

❖ Joshua's army marched around the walls of Jericho for seven days, and on the seventh day, seven times. The walls collapsed due to their shouts. (Joshua 6:15)

❖ The candelabrum (menorah) in the Temple had seven lamps. (Exodus 25:37) It's perhaps the most ancient symbol of the Israelites and is today the national emblem of the State of Israel.

❖ In Pharaoh's dream he saw seven healthy cows, seven sick

cows, seven heads of healthy grain, seven heads of scorched grains, seven years of plenty and seven years of famine. (Genesis 41:25)

❖ To celebrate their freedom from Egyptian slavery, God instructed the Israelites to eat unleavened bread for seven days. (Exodus 13:3-10)

❖ There are seven things God detests. (Proverbs 6:16-19)

❖ The House of Wisdom has Seven Pillars. (Proverbs 9:1)

❖ Jesus fed four thousand people with seven loafs of bread and seven basketfuls remaining. (Matthew 15:32-37)

❖ Jesus tells Peter to forgive his brethren seventy-seven times. (Matthew 18:21)

❖ Jesus is seventy-seventh in genealogical line from God. (Luke 3:23-38)

❖ Jesus uttered 'seven last words' or 'sayings' while on the cross.[178]

It is clear from many of the above examples that the number seven is a kind of symbolic approximation. For instance, Jesus's instruction to forgive 77 times is not an instruction to keep an exact count of people's transgressions and then pound them on their 78th. He simply meant people should forgive without tiring. Forgiving this way was holy.

In ancient India, too, through association with the configuration of the cosmic egg, the number seven was favored to represent many objects and events. Throughout the passages of the Rig Veda we find seven rivers, seven sages, seven regions, seven Suns, seven rays, seven wheeled cart, seven germs, seven horses/steeds, seven tongues, seven singers, seven castles, seven threads, seven reins, seven meters, seven floods, seven priests, seven treasures, seven cows, seven spears, seven splendors, seven glories, seven friends, seven portions, seven communities, seven mothers, and many more objects counted in multiples of seven.

Back to the fourteen realms.

You may have been surprised to learn at the end of the last section that the belief God created seven heavens and seven earths wasn't limited to the Israelite or Yogic tradition; that it was believed across many cultures.

About 1000 BC – around the period the Bible appeared – neighboring Sumerians, for instance, sang a hymn extolling seven earths and seven heavens, too.[179]

Interesting, too, is the fact that ancient Israelites, their neighbors, and also ancient Yogis far away in India believed there is a mystical path upwards through these seven heavens.[180] It was possible to reach God. But if you didn't have the required wisdom or 'password' you could get 'caught up' by angels or beautiful visions, and not reach the Lord who is in the highest heaven.[181]

This belief is implicit in a letter Paul wrote about an experience he had of heaven. (2 Corinthians 12.1-10) He recounts a spiritual journey wherein he got 'caught up into the third heaven.'

This is the only place in the Bible we find this curious phrase.

Everywhere else, writers refer to the 'heavens' (plural) or 'highest heaven,' which indicates plurality. The question arises: was Paul referring to the third heaven out of a tier of seven or was he referring to the third heaven as the highest of all?

Paul was a learned man. He mentions this in his letter. "I am not unskilled in knowledge. No, in every way we have been revealed to you in all things." (2 Corinthians 11.6) Thus, Paul would certainly have known that there were various versions of 3, 5, or 7 heavens. In such a situation, stating '3rd heaven' without explaining which version he was alluding to would have confused everyone. However, he had written to reveal his experience and clarify matters. But, he doesn't clarify the total number of heavens at all.

Why is this?

It's simply because he *didn't need to*. It wasn't new. His cosmology was well known.[182] He believed in seven heavens. To specify '3rd heaven' when he actually meant highest heaven is inconceivable. It would have misled everyone and defeated his purpose. Since there was no reason to do such a thing, it implies he was indeed talking of the third heaven amongst a scheme of seven. Since there were various schemata of heavens, 'Third heaven' and 'highest heaven' could not be used interchangeably.[183]

Remarkably, as you have seen, the overall 7+7 configuration of the Biblical cosmic world is not only the same as that of the nearby Sumerians but also the same as the distant Indian Yogis. Moreover, all were able to travel within those realms through spiritual prowess.

Spiritual experience is the same everywhere! Ancient seers around the world saw the same thing. Ancient spiritual traditions converge.

But this is not all. There are still many more converging cosmic descriptions of the Israelites and Yogis.

Come.

CONFLUENCE OF EAST AND WEST

YOU HAVE SEEN FOUR COMPELLING SETS of evidence attesting the description of creation in Genesis corresponds to the 'cosmic egg' of the Yogis. Here they are in brief:

1. The creation and characteristics of the cosmic egg in the Yoga Literature correspond to our Milky Way Galaxy. There are 42+18 = 60 convergences in all. Similarly, 21 major convergences appear when Genesis is compared to our Galaxy and Earth.

2. A core theme of the Yoga Literature is of God resting upon the primordial waters. It is here that the cosmic egg develops. A similar description of God presiding over primordial waters appears in Genesis. Here, too, is the location where the 'world' develops.

3. The Yoga Literature gives a detailed description of a Global Flood and Worldwide Extinction. It converges with science on 20 counts. The same cataclysmic episode is described briefly in Genesis.

4. Ancient Yogis and Israelites described God's creation as consisting of 3 and 14 realms.

On the first three major topics, Western and Eastern traditions converge marvelously with science and with each other. We have unification.

On the fourth topic, which is currently beyond the bounds of science, Western and Eastern traditions continue to converge with each other.

Total number of correspondences: twenty-two.

They aren't found in the Bible but in other ancient literature of the Israelites. The central corpus of this literature is called the 'Torah.' Traditionally, it is believed by Jews and Christians that God himself gave the Torah to Moses. He gave it in two forms. One written, the other oral. In its written form it comprises the first five books of the Bible beginning with Genesis. In its oral form it expands on events briefly described in the written form.[184]

Early Israelites believed it was crucial to study the oral tradition if you wished to understand the Bible and know God.[185] Moreover, the oral Torah concerning Creation and Genesis was regarded as the most ancient, original, and authentic[186] by early Israelites and Christians alike.

Later passages regarding rituals and legalities, however, did become an area of contention between the two groups.[187] Often called 'the law,' the word Torah actually means 'teaching' or 'instruction.'[188] Like most, Jesus himself very much accepted this tradition, at least in part. He was quite emphatic:

Don't think that I came to destroy the law
or the prophets.

I didn't come to destroy, but to fulfill.

For most certainly, I tell you,
until heaven and earth pass away,
not even one smallest letter or one tiny pen stroke
shall in any way pass away from the law,
until all things are accomplished.

Bible, Matthew 5:17-18

Today, unfortunately, the ancient oral tradition has slipped out of view. Later dogmas hog center stage. Proselytizing and propaganda sometimes seem to be the goal. Ancient cosmology has been forgotten. To me, that is where the spotlight should be shone.

Below, in Table 4, you will see exactly why. It's a compilation and comparison of what ancient Israelites, Christians, and Yogis believed about our cosmic world.[189]

	Cosmic Egg of Ancient Yogis	Cosmic World of Ancient Israelites & Christians
1	Created by God	Created by God
2	Comprises Fourteen Realms	Comprises Fourteen Realms
3	Each layered one above the other	Each layered one above the other
4	One earth + six heavens above	Seven heavens above
5	Seven underworlds below	Seven earths below

	Cosmic Egg of Ancient Yogis	Cosmic World of Ancient Israelites & Christians
6	Humankind is on the earth situated between the lowest heaven and highest underworld	Humankind is on the earth situated between the lowest heaven and second highest earth
7	Water above the highest heaven	Water above the highest heaven
8	Water below the lowest underworld	Water below the lowest earth
9	Water serves as the outer 'support'	Water serves as the outer 'support'
10	There is also water inside the unit. As such, the whole structure is surrounded by water and contains water	There is also water inside the unit. As such, the whole structure is surrounded by water and contains water
11	Fourteen Realms are within a single Unit	Fourteen Realms are within a single Unit
12	Highest heaven is reserved for the Creator	Highest heaven is reserved for the Creator
13	The heavens and earth + under-worlds form two halves that close upon each other like the two halves of an egg shell	The heavens and the earths form two halves that close upon each other like a teapot and its cover
14	The higher heavens are populated by spiritually advanced Yogis and pious souls	The higher heavens are populated by spiritually advanced angels, ministers, and pious souls, some born, others unborn
15	The lower earths are generally animalistic and materialistic	The lower earths are generally animalistic and materialistic
16	The cosmic structure arose in darkness	The cosmic structure arose in darkness
17	It evolved within water	It evolved within water

	Cosmic Egg of Ancient Yogis	Cosmic World of Ancient Israelites & Christians
18	God presided over those primordial waters	God presided over those primordial waters
19	He created three divisions in the cosmic structure at its center. They comprise heaven and earth separated by a firmament (The Three Realms)	He created three divisions in the cosmic structure at its center. They comprise heaven and earth separated by a firmament (The Three Realms)
20	Our Earth has witnessed six periodic cycles. The first five, like the sixth, may also have seen mass extinctions by volcanic activity and floods that wiped out nearly all life	Our Earth has witnessed six periodic mass extinctions by floods that wiped out nearly all life. Noah's flood was not the first
21	We live in the seventh era	We live in the seventh era
22	God created innumerable worlds and manifests in all of them. He is not localized to any religion on planet Earth. He is universal.	God created 18,000 worlds and manifests in all of them. He is not localized to any religion on planet Earth. He is universal.

Table 4: Twenty-two similarities between the cosmic realms of ancient Yogis, Israelites, and Christians.

All the above twenty-two characteristics of creation were shared by the ancient Yogis, Israelites, and Christians.

The implications are vast and numerous.

How can so many convergences occur by accident? There is no doubt that these traditions spoke of one and the same fourteen-layered Cosmic Egg. Indeed, it refers to our magnificent Milky Way Galaxy.

There are, nevertheless, some places where the descriptions digress slightly. This is to be expected since the ancient Sages and

215

Yogis would naturally have their own cultural traditions. For instance, you saw in Table 3 above that the Israelites count 7 heavens + 7 earths = 14 realms. The Yogis count 6 heavens + 1 earth + 7 underworlds = 14 realms. (Not to be confused with the encompassing units – the cosmic eggs – mentioned in comparison 22.) However, the Yogis regard the six heavens and central earth under one banner called a *vyahriti*. This therefore divides the *brahmanda* into seven upper and seven lower realms just like the belief of the early Israelites and Christians.

The reason why the Yogis grouped the earth with the six heavens is because it has the potential to be a heaven! It can be a Paradise, if we allow it. Indeed, under the system of eras the Yogis described (Workshop 1), the first in the cycle is called the *Satya Yuga*. This is the 'Age of Truth.' During this blessed period, there is no evil or affliction. Earth is a Paradise. It's like heaven.

Perhaps, what is most rewarding to learn from the oral tradition of the ancient Israelites is that they believed that God created thousands of worlds, not just our planet Earth, and that he visits all of them, interacting with all his creatures.[190] The belief that, in the whole wide universe God belongs only to some religious groups on our tiny planet, is a new one. Early Israelites didn't believe this. They said he is universal.

It may be said that He [God] rides a light cherub,
and floats in eighteen thousand worlds;
for it is said,

The chariots of God are myriads ... .
He is sporting with the leviathan ... .

Yes, He sports with His creatures ... .

Abodah Zarah, 3b, 22, 11, 13[191]

This understanding that God belongs to all is similar to that of the ancient Yogis. God manifests as Avatars in innumerable forms, in innumerable places, within innumerable cosmic eggs, whenever he so desires.

He belongs to *everyone* and *everything*. He is Universal.

God resides eternally
within his transcendental abode,
and while residing there, he,
wherever, to whomever,
in whichever form he deems appropriate, reveals himself;
and to whomever it is appropriate he speaks,
and to whomever it is appropriate he touches.

Just as an accomplished Yogi seated in one place
can see for thousands of leagues[192]
or can listen to conversations thousands of leagues away,
similarly God, while remaining
in his transcendental abode
reveals himself [simultaneously]
in infinite cosmic eggs
wherever and however it is appropriate

GOD IS REAL

and remains eternally in his abode.

Vachanamruta, Gadhada II.64

I will now show you the last and most amazing convergence of the Bible and Yoga Literature (and other traditions).

It's also the most ancient.

CONVERGING COSMOLOGIES

YOU JUST SAW THAT THE BELIEF in seven heavens and seven earths, and the ability to travel through them, wasn't unique to the Yogis and Israelites. It may not surprise you, then, to learn that their belief in a cosmic egg wasn't unique, either.

It was common to a number of ancient traditions including Chinese, Egyptian, Finnish, and Greek.[193] However, the notion of it representing the body of the Lord's first Avatar – the macranthropus Purusha seems only to have taken root in India and Greece. The Indian theme, which is highly intricate, has correspondences with an ancient Greek religion called Orphism. It flourished around 600 BC. It is assumed that the sage Orpheus was its founder. Unfortunately, very little information about him or his religion survives.

We know that the Orphics believed in a cosmic egg which gave birth to a first being, like Brahma, called Phanes or Protogonos. The great god Zeus swallowed Phanes and became a macranthropus himself.

Like the Purusha of the Rig Veda, Zeus's body contains the whole world. His head represents the heavens and his two eyes are the Sun and Moon. Unlike the Rig Veda, his arms, belly, and feet aren't represented. His description seems fragmentary or partially lost.

Clearly, belief in a cosmic egg was very much a part of many ancient traditions, particularly Yoga, Judaism, Christianity, and Orphism. It was a widespread, and quite probably, worldwide spiritual experience.

Most importantly, it shows traditions whose teachers had similar cosmic experiences must have taught similar cosmologies and therefore, also, similar theologies. Their terminologies, of-course, will have been various. These core similarities we have witnessed between ancient cosmologies (and their implied theologies) of the world's great traditions are profound.

Finally, we will round up all the convergences between the Bible and ancient Yoga Literature with a look at the following hymn.

Along with the *Purusha Sukta* depicting the Lord's Sacrifice and the creation from it of 3 and 14 realms, another ancient creation hymn of importance in the Rig Veda is the *Nasadiya Sukta*. It's a philosophical discussion of creation by a Yogi who finally jests even God may not know how everything came to be. This comment has inspired generations of interpretations and debates!

You will probably find parts of this ancient description of the world and its primordial image strikingly familiar.

Here is the hymn.

In the beginning
there was neither existence nor non-existence;
then the world was not, not the firmament,
nor the heaven above it ... .

How could there be
any investing envelope [of the egg[194]], and where?

How could there be the deep, unfathomable water?
There was darkness covered by darkness in the beginning,
all this [world] was indistinguishable water,
that empty united [world]
which was covered by a mere nothing [space], was produced ... .

Who really knows? Who in this world may declare
from where was this creation? ...

He from whom this creation arose,
he may uphold it, or he may not;
he who is its superintendent in the highest heaven,
he assuredly knows, or if he knows not [no one else does].

Rig Veda Samhita, Nasadiya Sukta, 10.129

Clearly, some Yogis very much enjoyed teasing their students. And as you saw earlier, they defended, "Divinities are fond of the cryptic and dislike the evident."[195] They rarely handed things on a plate.

But take a close look at the third paragraph. What is this ancient, abyssal, watery, dark, empty, 'united' world described by the Yogis? The object is clearly the primordial cosmic egg. It is none other than the structure described on Day 1 in Genesis – an unfathomable abyss of water covered in darkness awaiting the creation of earth, firmament, and heaven, the 3-tiered Realm. Genesis 1.1 and this important passage in *Nasadiya Sukta* are almost identical in substance.

Again, the implications are vast and numerous.

There can be no doubt the Israelites and Yogis spoke of the very same cosmic egg! Their beliefs mirrored each other. They described exactly the same cosmic structure. *They shared a cosmology.* Therefore, they should also have shared a theology. East and West converged.

There must have been a time in the distant past when the earliest sages of Israel and India – as well as other teachers from other traditions as far apart as Greece and China – all experienced and taught essentially the same thing.

The differences you see in these traditions today are superficial. They are a result of evolving times, needs, and culture. But predominantly, in my view, they have arisen because there are also different ways of connecting with God. Various rituals, various prayers and devotions, various pilgrimages, holy icons, festivals, and places of worship. Innovations are limitless. Today, people are even using the internet – whatever works. Beneath the surface, the differences are minimal.

Does this imply spiritual experience is similar everywhere?

Certainly.

From whichever tradition you may hail, and wherever you may be in the world, indeed, in the universe, if you practice the core principles of Faith, Prayer, and Yoga, you will experience the same cosmos and God.

The existence of these convergences between Eastern and Western traditions provides a foundation for an all-embracing, universal spiritual outlook and an appreciation for all spiritual traditions – whatever our own preference. Religious 'exclusivism' – the imperialist and chauvinistic idea that one's own spiritual beliefs form the only true religion and that all other groups are delinquent – is misconceived. Indeed, quite the opposite turns out to be true: spiritual inclusivism and universalism. We are all truly climbing different faces of the same mountain. Its highest peak is the destination we all seek.

The new convergences from all directions between apparently disparate spiritual traditions and also between them and modern science establish a worthy starting point for this universal, all-inclusive spirituality. The convergences can help bring about reciprocal regard and respect; ending of antagonism and arrogance; the beginning of a new dialogue of peace, reconciliation, and unification.

There will be hurdles, but this is a splendid place to start.

The well-known phrase 'to be in seventh heaven' when describing a very happy person, derives from the ancient belief in seven heavens and seven earths. That blissful seventh heaven can be brought to Earth when we realize the convergence of scientific discovery and widespread spiritual experience, the fact that a caring God truly exists, and that he belongs to all life forms in the universe, to all creatures great and small. God is Universal.

CONCLUSION: GOD IS REAL

THERE IS NO CONFLICT BETWEEN science and ancient spirituality. The colossal convergences, and also those between Eastern and Western spiritual traditions of antiquity, cannot be ignored. They demonstrate the authenticity and universality of spiritual experience.

They are also powerful evidence for the existence of God and *his* universality. He belongs to all beings and can be approached by all people. He is accessible to all.

The numerous new correspondences are a game-changer in the 'science versus spirituality' debate. Science and spirituality converge! The new discoveries uphold the various beliefs in spirituality, ancient scripture, and God's existence.

As you saw earlier in the case of Emma despairingly losing her ten year old Daniel to cancer, times of personal loss, injury, untimely death of a loved one – all these and so much more can bring even the strongest to doubt God's existence. So much so, they can bring them to the brink of self-destruction.

But God's loving presence is truly established by these major convergences. And, knowing that God exists, that he cares for you, and loves you brings profound peace. Realizing that he not only loves you, but is right here *within* you opens fountains of joy! God dotes over you like a loving parent over a child! The uniqueness with God, however, is that he does it from within you, and within every creature in the universe! God is not small. He is not a cosmic man. He is a universal being. His essence is *love*.

After receiving this book and reading about these truths now so clearly proven from the Bible and Yoga Literature, Emma realized God's loving presence within her, too, and she returned to peace and happiness. Crucial to the needs of many people like her today, some who may be sitting on the fence, and others standing at a crossroad unable to decide which way to go, the numerous convergences demonstrate God's existence and his love within us all. In a single sweep, they reveal the objective and verifiable Truth of ancient scripture and the authenticity of our ancient spiritual teachers.

Doubts about God's existence or love can also occur when a person feels the suffering *of others*, or witnesses mass deaths, and tribulation due to political oppression or natural disaster. "If God exists why does he allow so much pain, suffering, and injustice? Why is there a rise in terrorism, violence, bullying, road rage, and other malignancies? Why doesn't he answer all our prayers?" These are just some of the causes for doubt many believers go through, be they orthodox believers or casual followers.

The truth is, some of these maladies arise because we have lost our bearings. Some things in the world happen not due to God, but due to ourselves when we move away from our center. Forgetting our spiritual essence, we have become increasingly physical and material. We have become biological machines in the proverbial rat race. We lose sight of the long term and all that is truly dear to us. In many ways, we seem also to be destroying our planet.

The problem with man is not God, religion, nor politics, nor anything else per se. The problem with man, is *man*. Men, women, and children are forgetting their spiritual identity. It can be a downward slope. Losing this crucial centerpoint, a person can become inhumane. The person abuses his or her freewill.

Freewill is the most loving gift God can give: Total Freedom! But with total freedom arises the need for great restraint.

Most people have it. But sadly, a small percentage deliberately cross the bounds of civility for their selfish pursuits. On the other hand, focusing on their own true identity and the realization that a loving God exists within every creature on Earth, can make them sublime. Most importantly, applying it to their daily lives brings peace not only to themselves but to the people around them. The whole world can become a better place.

Yet, we do not have all the answers to all questions. There is so much we have yet to understand. It takes introspection, time, and experience. Sometimes it takes a lifetime. Sometimes, a solitary moment of insight.

Be that as it may, one thing is certain: Our ancient spiritual teachers were not mistaken. Their assertion that God exists, and that he is good, loving, and just, is *True*. The numerous and detailed descriptions of deep-sea volcanoes, hydrothermal vents, ancient worldwide extinction and flooding, our Galaxy, the universe, the Big Bang, and so much more you have seen given by the world's wisest sages in the Bible and Yoga Literature demonstrate their authenticity and honesty beyond doubt. The inner spiritual path that led them to discover our universe and describe it in magnificent detail, also led them to discover God. When they said "God exists, is within you, and loves you," they spoke from direct experience.

Previously, the revered passages of the world's most ancient texts were perceived to be naive descriptions of the universe and an imaginary, mythic God. Some skeptics have deliberately or unwittingly misled people with their comments on these ancient texts. In doing so, they have hurt the scientific venture by devaluing their personal trustworthiness in the eyes of many people. The scientist who denied a correlation between the ancient Yoga Literature and salt-removing hydrothermal vents is a case to remember.

Some years back, at a national convention where I was invited to speak before about 5,000 people, I asked a youth, "Do you believe in science?" His answer was swift. "I believe in science, but I don't believe in scien*tists*." He pretty well summed up the general perception of scientists amongst many people today. The blatantly unfair, one-eyed, and vicious attacks by some scientists on spirituality have hurt their credibility. The question that results in the minds of many people is, "Which scientists can we trust? How many are telling us the complete truth?"

Nevertheless, in some cases, these biased attacks aren't wholly the fault of skeptics. They're merely evaluating the ancient passages according to their knowledge at the time. As an illiterate or ignorant person viewing words or symbols written on a piece of paper might perceive them as meaningless scribbles or artwork, similarly, some people genuinely misunderstand the Bible and Yoga Literature. Oblivious of new discoveries, they assume the ancient descriptions of the universe are naive speculation composed into poetry, and finally recorded as spirituality. Fortunately, the progress of science has led from one discovery to another, and has enabled us to understand and piece together the cryptic revelations of the ancient Yogis and inspirers of the Bible.

Originally, skeptics used to argue that spiritual people don't understand science. Today, the opposite is true. Skeptics don't understand spirituality – and they have no excuse. The new evidence for spirituality and God's existence is *objective*. They need to do their homework and read up on what they don't know. They should pull their heads out of the sand and open their eyes, and if possible their minds, to view these major new convergences. Indeed, the history of science is replete with discoveries that have forced scientists to review and transform their deepest beliefs about the universe. Each time they embraced the new discoveries, they grew. Now again, they have the opportunity to grow.

The number of correspondences between modern science and ancient spirituality in this book total 121. Nineteen of these are numerical. It's unthinkable they can arise by chance. From these, seven concern timelines and accurately give them for volcanic activity in the southern Indian Ocean, a global extinction and flood, development of our Galaxy's halo and disk, its lifespan, as well as the end of our Earth and Sun. How can all these major timelines be guessed correctly by chance? They are impossible to guess because there are an infinite number of potential answers – any number of years whatsoever between one and infinity.

So, as I have summed up before, if there is just one thing you should remember, it's this: there are *too many convergences to be a coincidence.* The finest minds in the world such as Plato, Ptolomy, Aristotle, Galileo, and Newton *combined* were unable to arrive at even a fraction of all this knowledge. Neither was it even possible to access this knowledge of the universe without the use of advanced mathematical theorems and sophisticated instruments. Its extensive presence in ancient spiritual texts therefore demands another explanation. The rational and only remaining one is the *spiritual* one, as explicitly explained by the ancient sages and yogis themselves!

The convergences are both descriptive and numerical, and lead us to the inescapable conclusion that they cannot be by chance. They are not the product of fantasy or speculation. The Yogis described both the timeframes and related events unambiguously. They are undeniable evidence of the knowledge and wisdom of our ancient teachers and the authenticity of their message.[196]

We also discovered there are at least 22 similarities between the cosmic beliefs of the ancient Yogis, Israelites, and Christians. Their spiritual experiences converge.

Taken together with the love, care, and altruism of those ancient teachers, all this combines to provide a concrete bedrock upon which almost anyone can build a richer spiritual life. A life of goodwill, charity, and understanding. A heart of compassion, forgiveness, and love. And a soul of prayer, purity, and stillness. The ancient sages certainly understood the subjects they spoke about. They could see our entire universe in all its dimensions as it exists today. They could even see its remotest past and furthest future.

Importantly, they could see much more: the spiritual, transcendental world. These are realms that will always reside beyond the sights of telescopes and the networks of human brains. If only humanity could lend a devout ear to their core message that a caring, all-embracing universal God exists, it would bring deep tranquility to every soul.

There is no doubt a higher, loving spiritual power exists, call it 'God,' 'Energy,' 'Prime Mover,' or anything else. Many people already know this from personal, spiritual experience or other special events in their lives. Others adhere to the belief as a matter of faith. However, more and more people are seeking scientific or rational justification for their beliefs. An increasing number of well-meaning people, particularly youth, are being pushed away from their spiritual beliefs due to the negative repercussions of some religious regimes around the world and the circulation of atheistic material in various media. There is also a spreading cloud of atheism and an attack on all things spiritual. These youths are also being told by some so-called intellectuals that descriptions of creation and the universe in ancient scripture do not correspond to reality, that they have no soul, there is no God, and there is no evidence for God. That it is all fantasy or speculation at best. That there is no heaven apart from a selfish hedonist one we might make on Earth. Prayers are to an empty sky, they say. Faith must be placed in them, not God.

Such ideas are gradually taking root and are in many ways themselves a contributor to the world's problems. At least, they don't make them easier.

The truth is, faith and prayer are the *life* of our world! Their energy and reach cannot be imagined. Faith and prayer have saved humanity from ruin innumerable times and they will continue to do so. Indeed, if there is but one solution to the challenges of the future, it is Spirituality. Reverence for each other, reverence for all life, and reverence for the whole universe can only come from a spiritual outlook on life.

This is why, though the agitation and discontentment of thoughtful people is legitimate and should continue till the world's problems are properly resolved, their unrest should not spill over into doubting the authenticity of their ancient teachers. The problem with spirituality isn't with its founders, but with selfish and corrupt humans who have distorted their sublime message.

The amazing new convergences of science and spirituality will prove helpful to all spiritual people, as well as this growing young population. The convergences also help resolve the perennial question, "Why are all the religions so different?" We can see now that they aren't. Many bear fundamental similarities. They are very much the same beneath the surface.

Follow your Faith. Reach out to your religion. Expand your consciousness. Grow closer to God. Everyone is climbing the same proverbial mountain, albeit up different faces, according to the traditions and cultural heritage of their own Faith. The basic elements of them, as you have seen, are the same.

Therefore do not aim to convert others. If you delve inwards, you will probably find you need to work on yourself. Self-improvement is a lifelong, ever-continuing endeavor, and is the most powerful way to teach.

Each and every human being in the world needs to take responsibility for their own spiritual growth. Despite the seemingly chaotic state of the world today, this will happen in due course as more and more people draw closer to enlightenment in every sector of society, and most importantly, within the individual family.

Heed the inner voice beckoning you towards the transcendental. Focus upon it and seek its source. Do not ignore it or shut it from your mind. Embrace it. Absorb it. Revel in it. It's both the path and the goal. Do you need to change your religion to do this? No. Reach out to your own tradition with the spirit in which it was revealed by its founder or any of its humanitarian leaders. Anyone who inspires you. You may find that that is your own father or mother, whom you have seen to practice the message more than any preacher you know. Or it may be a friend, or a child. Become, as far as you can, the image of that person. Not in appearance, but in behavior and belief. If you cannot follow this principle in your current religion, it's unlikely you will find it easier in any other religion you may convert to.

Remember, you're likely to find all sorts of people, whichever spiritual group you subscribe to: Those who are pious, others who are liberal, and some who are hypocrites. Do not let the latter bother you. As in school, college, and university you find sincere as well as insincere students, so you will find them in spirituality, too. But as you do not renounce your school or university because of these students, do not renounce your opportunity for spiritual growth and enlightenment in your own spiritual tradition.

So much is tied to your spiritual growth. It's your lifeline. Long-term worldly success can proceed from it, too, because spiritual growth builds self-esteem and confidence. It helps you bounce back when things are tough. Spirituality forges a powerful and positive response to all challenges. It can strengthen your family, improve your health, help you grow financially, and enhance your sense of well-being. It's the single most important influence behind achieving your dreams. Even better, spirituality can help you expand and grow yourself *beyond* your dreams!

You have seen that yoga is a powerful catalyst of spiritual growth and personal harmony. It helps you expand your consciousness. It enables you to go beyond faith and belief into the realm of *experience*. Nothing trumps this. Nothing erodes it. Nothing shakes you from it. You experience a surge of joy and a transition from believing, to *Knowing*. This is my own experience and it can be yours, too. Indeed, it may already be so.

Importantly, yoga isn't a religion, but it's where all religions can meet. Indeed, the discoveries in this book reveal that it's where the whole universe meets. Yoga is a science in its own right, the universal science of spirituality. And yoga is leverage – physical, mental, emotional, and spiritual. Not only can it make you healthier, it can enhance and strengthen your daily spiritual practice. Most importantly, it can bring you peace of mind and take you closer to God, whichever spiritual tradition you belong to.

Yoga opens your heart!

There are many truths in the spiritual literature of the world's great religions. Reach out to your Faith and reach into your Soul. The Secrets of the Grand Cosmos, the Sovereign Lord, and the Meaning of Life are within you. Allow them to breathe and blossom. Faith, Prayer, and Yoga are their nourishment. You are their repository. Discover pure *Bliss!*

AS I BRING THIS FIRST VOLUME to a close, I would like to say something about the future. It isn't so much about whether governments, the media, politics, or economics will change the world. In the age of the Internet, it's more a question of whether the individual will make an extra effort to uphold the truths of spirituality. Through the Internet, I believe he and she will. Many individuals like yourself who are aware of these new convergences already do.

I believe 2012 will be a pivotal year in the history of humankind. Not because the world will end, but because many individuals will spiritually awake and take their experience to the Internet.

Already, millions of people around the world are rising to the cause of truth, freedom, fairness, and justice. Indeed, humankind is headed toward a new kind of Spirituality, Consciousness, and

Knowledge that will herald a new world Understanding. It will gather more and more momentum from 2012 as the collective consciousness of millions of individuals approaches a critical mass. It will precipitate an unstoppable wave. However, just as mass extinctions don't have a single cause but usually a group of them, similarly mass awakenings emerge for a cluster of reasons: environmental upheaval; realization of the disrespect we have had for our planet and life in general; dietary change – we are what we eat and drink; and the growing awareness of not only the major convergences between science and spirituality, but also between Eastern and Western spiritual traditions.

All this will create a Great Flood, not of water, but of spiritual awareness spreading across numerous continents, in 2012.

HOW YOU CAN HELP

IMAGINE A BEAUTIFUL WORLD RID of religious exclusivism. Imagine our planet awash with the mutual respect of science and spirituality. Imagine people of many Faiths flocking together. All this is truly possible and *you* have the power to make it happen. It's possible with the knowledge you hold in your palms right now.

Please discuss these new convergences with as many people as you can. So much in the world can become better because of *You*. We all need to do our part. We're all in this together.

Following is my mission. Thousands have joined already. Please join us, too. We need you. The *world* needs you.

1. Bring peace and happiness to all by spreading the new proof of God's existence and love.
2. Promote interfaith harmony by discussing the similarities between Eastern and Western traditions.
3. Grow and expand personally through the power of spirituality.

Together We Can Do This.

Thank you for your support.

Don't forget to sign up and join at
www.SanjayCPatel.com

for latest updates, newsletters, podcasts, blogs, and seminars.

Don't forget to tell your friends!
Follow me on Twitter and Facebook!

www.twitter.com/SanjayCPatel

www.facebook.com/www.SanjayPatel.co

www.SanjayCPatel.com

UPCOMING NEW BOOK !

DON'T MISS IT !

Thank you for spending your precious time reading through these new convergences. I hope you found them valuable. But the trail doesn't end here. There are still many more exciting correspondences between Science and Spirituality! They will appear in my upcoming second book. They concern the Earth, Sun, Space, Atom, and Infinity to mention a few. You won't be disappointed. Don't miss it!

For updates, please sign up at www.SanjayCPatel.com.

Ten percent of all royalties in this series of books and seminars go to charity.

Sanjay's *Signature* Seminars

Sanjay has been conducting workshops and seminars for twenty years, helping thousands of individuals to grow personally, financially, and spiritually. He has conducted nearly 5,000 workshops and seminars, attended by more than 67,000 people, and addressed audiences of up to 3,000 attendees at mega events.

He has also conducted numerous seminars for medical fraternities, educational organizations, businesses, and other organizations, where he has received standing ovations. Yoga, Meditation, and Simple Lifestyle Change compose the center of his powerful, life-transforming seminars.

You, too, can expand and grow yourself beyond your dreams!

To enroll or for more information visit:

www.SanjayCPatel.com

About Sanjay

In 2004, Sanjay C. Patel became the first person in the world to present *objective* proof of God based on ancient spiritual texts and a fully scientifically compatible explanation of Genesis's 7 Days and the Flood in 2007. Patel's explanation is rational, complete, coherent, and in line with mainstream science.

Sanjay is a pioneer and leading expert in the field of comparative ancient and modern cosmology. Unprecedentedly, his research demonstrating major convergences between modern science and ancient spiritual texts has been published in three international science journals. The paradigm-breaking research concerns deep-sea volcanoes, hydrothermal vents, and identical objects named *Vadavanala Agni* by ancient Yogis. His new discoveries were also presented at the *22nd International Congress of History of Science* at Beijing, China, July 2005, where they were warmly received.

Sanjay is an independent scholar with thirty years of study and experience in the field of spirituality. He also studied in a traditional setting as a monk for five intensive years at an ashram in India. Subjects of his study included Theology, Sanskrit, Yoga, and Ancient Cosmology. They form the early foundation of this book.

During this time he also learned the ancient art of Yoga and Meditation from a Master and practiced it fives times a day for decades. His dedicated practice led to an inner awakening that revealed the spiritual oneness of all people and all great spiritual traditions.

In response to his deeply touching experiences, Sanjay embarked upon a mission to help others connect with their own spirituality and experience its priceless rewards. He has traveled extensively throughout the world with his message of achieving personal success and experiencing joy through yoga and simple lifestyle changes. In August 2004, he delivered an enlightening talk on Work-Life Balance to 600 medical doctors at a seminar in Chicago where the bestselling author Deepak Chopra, M.D. was also a speaker.

BIBLIOGRAPHY

Note

TRANSLATIONS, SOURCES CITED
OR RECOMMENDED READING

The literature containing the remarkable convergences of science and spirituality is sometimes longwinded and contains descriptions of theological and mystical concepts not of importance to the present study. These portions have mostly been removed from the passages quoted in this book. Furthermore, previous translations of the ancient literature sometimes reflect assumptions by the translator. Most of the passages in this book have therefore been retranslated from the original Sanskrit, literally word for word, by competent and recognized Sanskrit scholars to remove these assumptions and reveal the ancient passages exactly as they are. (They will be published shortly in a separate volume. Please visit www.SanjayCPatel.com for updates.) Furthermore, because these literal translations are sometimes difficult to read smoothly, some passages have been reconstructed in the current publication to improve their readability. The passages presented are not intended in any way to reflect the opinions of the translators, nor to be understood as verbatim extracts from their translations, though they may sometimes be so. I have included references to the original texts to facilitate study of previous translations readily available to the public. The source for quotes derived from the Bible is the *World English Bible* which is in the public domain, http://ebible.org/web/. My discussions of and references to scientific material are likewise for the express purpose of criticism and review only.

SCIENTIFIC LITERATURE

Adams, A. & Laughlin, G. (2006). *The Five Ages of the Universe.*
Angel, R.B. (1980). *Relativity: The Theory and Its Philosophy.*
Atkins, P. W. (1993). *Creation Revisited.*
Barrow, J.D. & Tipler, F. J. (1988). *The Anthropic Cosmological Principle.*
Barrow, J.D. & Silk, J. (1994). *The Left Hand of Creation.*
Bartusiak, M. (2006). *Archives of the Universe. New York, N.Y: Vintage*
Begelman, M. & Rees, M. (1996). *Gravity's Fatal Attraction.*
Bell, J.S. (2004). *Speakable and Unspeakable in Quantum Mechanics.*
Benson, H. (2000). *The Relaxation Response.*
Bhaskara II. (1072). *The Siddhanta Shiromani.* Translated by Lancelot
Wilkinson and revised by Bapu Deva Shastri. (1861).
Binney, J. & Tremaine, S. (2008). *Galactic Dynamics.*
Brown, M. & Rushmer, T. (2008). *Evolution and Differentiation of the Continental Crust,* Cambridge University Press
Carroll, B. & and Ostlie, D. (2007). *An Introduction to Modern Astrophysics.*
Collins, F.S. (2006). *The Language of God.*
Croswell, K. (2000). *The Alchemy of the Heavens.*
Ferris, T. (2003). *Coming of Age in the Milky Way. New York: HarperCollins Publishers, Inc.*
Goldsmith, D. (1997). *Einstein's Greatest Blunder?*
Hawking, S.W. (1998). *A Brief History of Time.*
Hellemans, A. & Bunch, B. (1991). *The Timetables of Science.*
Horgan, J. (1998). *The End of Science.*
Kaku, K. (1995). *Hyperspace.*
Kaler, J. B. (2006). *The Cambridge Encyclopedia of Stars.*
Kanigel, R. (1991). *The Man Who Knew Infinity.*
Karttunen, H; Kroger, P; Oja, H; Poutanen, M; Donner, K. J. (2006). *Fundamental Astronomy.*
Kitchin, C. R. (1990). *Journeys to the Ends of the Universe.*
Longair, M. (2008). *Galaxy Formation.*
Morrison, D. & Wolff, S.C. (1994). *Frontiers of Astronomy.*
Myers, D.G. (2005). *Social Psychology.*
Peebles, P.J.E. (1993). *Principles of Physical Cosmology.*
Penrose, R. (2002). *The Emperor's New Mind.*
Radin, D. (1997). *The Conscious Universe.*
Rees, M.J. (2001). *Just Six Numbers: The Deep Forces That Shape the Universe.*
Rogers, J.J.W. & Santosh, M. *Continents and Supercontinents,* (2004), Oxford University Press
Roos, M. (2003). *Introduction to Cosmology.*
Rowan-Robinson, M. (2004). *Cosmology.*
Roy, A.E. & Clarke, D. (1989). *Astronomy – Structure of the Universe.*
Schneider, P. (2006). *Extragalactic Astronomy and Cosmology.*
Stewart, I. (1990). *Does God Play Dice?*

Tayler, R.J. (2003). *Galaxies: Structure and Evolution.*
Unsöld, A., Baschek, B. & and Brewer, W.D. (2005). *The New Cosmos.*
van Fraassen, B.C. (1991). *Quantum Mechanics: An Empiricist View.*
Walker, C. (1996). *Astronomy Before the Telescope.*
Watson, P. (2005). Ideas. *New York, NY: HarperCollins Publishers.*
Weinberg, S. (2008). *Cosmology.*
Zeilik, M., Gregory, S.A. & Smith, E.P. (1997). *Introductory Astronomy and Astrophysics.*

SPIRITUAL LITERATURE

Aitareya Upanishad, from The Thirteen Principle Upanishads, translated by
  Hume, R.E. (1983). Oxford University Press: Delhi
Agnimahapuranam, translated by Dutt, M. N., edited by Joshi, K. L. (2001). Pari-
  mal Publications: Delhi
Baskalamantra-Upanishad, edited by Ježic, M. in his edition Rigvedske upanišadi:
  Aitareya, Kaushitaki, Baskalamantra-upanishad, Zagreb: Matica Hrvatska, (1999).
Bible, Interlinear, Hebrew, Greek, English, by Jay P. Green. (1984).
Bible, New American Standard Bible, translated by a board
  of scholars. (1995).
Bible, New International Version, translated by a board of scholars. (1978).
Bible, Young's Literal Translation, By Robert Young. (1898).
Bible, Interlinear Scripture Analyzer, http://www.scripture4all.org
Bible, Torah Transliteration Scripture,
  *http://www.messianic-torah-truth-seeker.org/Scriptures/Tenakh/Barasheet/ge001.h
  tm*
Bhagavad Gita, by Shivananda S.
Bhagavad Geeta, Geeta Press, Gorakhpur.
Brahma Purana, translated by a board of scholars, (2001). Motilal Banarasidass Pub-
  lishers: Delhi
Brahmanda Purana, translated by a board of scholars, edited by Shastri, J.L.
  (1983). Motilal Banarsidass Publishers: Delhi
Brihadaranyaka Upanishad, from The Thirteen Principle Upanishads,
  translated by Hume, R.E. (1983). Oxford University Press: Delhi
Chhandogya Upanishad, from The Thirteen Principle Upanishads,
  translated by Hume, R.E. (1983). Oxford University Press: Delhi
Hindu Realism, Chatterji, J.C. (1912).
Introduction to the Pancaratra and Ahirbudhnya Samhita, Schrader, F.O. (1916).
Ishavasya Upanishad, from The Thirteen Principle Upanishads, translated by
  Hume, R.E. (1983). Oxford University Press: Delhi
Katha Upanishad, from The Thirteen Principle Upanishads, translated by Hume, R.E.
  (1983). Oxford University Press: Delhi
Kirtan Muktavali, Swaminarayan Akshar Pith. (2003).
Kurma Purana, translated by Tagare, G. V., (2005). Motilal Banarasidass Publishers:
  Delhi
Legends of the Jews, Volume I, *'Bible Times and Characters from the Creation to Ja-
  cob,'* by Ginzberg, L., (1909). Forgotten Books.
Mahabharata of Krishna-Dwaipayana Vyasa, translated by Ganguli, K.M. (1883 and
  1896).
Markandeya Purana, translated by Pargiter, F.E., edited by Joshi, K.L. (2004). Parimal
  Publications: Delhi
Markandeya Puranam, translated by Dutt, M.N., edited by Kumar, P. (2005). Eastern
  Book Linkers: Delhi
Markandeya Purana, translated by Pargiter, F.E., edited by Joshi, K.L. (2004). Parimal
  Publications: Delhi

Matsya Mahapurana, translated by a board of scholars, edited by Joshi, K.L. (2007). Parimal Publications: Delhi

Ramayana, by Valmiki, Gita Press.

Rig Veda Samhita, translation according to Wilson, H.H. & Bhashya of Sayanacharya, edited by Arya, R.P. & Joshi, K.L. (2005). Parimal Publications: Delhi

Rig Veda, translated by Griffith, R.T.H. (1896).

Shikshapatri, by Shri Swaminarayan, Swaminarayan Akshar Pith. (2002).

Siva Mahapurana, translated by Nagar, S.L. (2007). Parimal Publications: Delhi

Shreemad Bhagavata Maha Purana, translated by Goswami, C.L. & Shastri, M.A. (2005). Gita Press: Gorakhpur

Shvetashvatara Upanishad, from The Thirteen Principle Upanishads, translated by Hume, R.E. (1983). Oxford University Press: Delhi

Skanda Purana, translated by a board of scholars, edited by Bhatt, G. P. (1992). Motilal Banarasidass Publishers: Delhi

Sri Ramacaritamanasa, Gita Press, Gorakhpur, India

Swamini Vatu, Gunatitananda S., (2002). Swaminarayan Akshar Pith, Amdavad

Surya Siddhanta – a Text-Book of Hindu Astronomy, translated by Burgess, E., edited by Gangooly, P. (2005). Motilal Banarasidass Publishers: Delhi

The Upanishads, translations by Sri Aurobindo. (1996).

Vachanamruta, by Shri Swaminarayan, compiled by Muktananda, S., Gopalananda, S., Nityananda, S. & Shukananda, S., Swaminarayan Akshar Pith. (1996).

Vayu Purana, translated by a board of scholars, Tagare, G.V., edited by Bhatt, G. P. and Shastri, J.L. (2003). Motilal Banarasidass Publishers: Delhi

Vedras, by Shri Swaminarayan, in Gujarati, Yogi Printery. (1978).

Vishnu Purana, translated by Wilson, H.H., edited by Singh, N.S. (2003). Nag Publishers: Delhi

Wisdom of Vaisheshika, Bahadur, K.P. (1979).

Yajur Veda, Taittiriya Samhita.

Yoga Sutras of Patanjali, translated by Sachidananda, S. (2005). Integral Yoga Publications: Virginia

Yoga Vasishta of Valmiki, translated by Mitra, V.L., edited by Arya, R.P.

Dictionaries:

Cologne Digital Sanskrit Lexicon (from Monier-Williams, *'Sanskrit-English Dictionary' 2008*). http://webapps.uni-koeln.de/tamil/

Sanskrit-English Dictionary, Revised edition, Oxford University Press, Monier-Williams, M (1989).

The Old Testament Hebrew Lexicon (Brown, Driver, Briggs, Gesenius) http://www.biblestudytools.net/Lexicons/Hebrew/

Bhagavad Gomandal, by a board of scholars, (1985).

243

IMAGE CREDITS

Figure 1.1. Derived from janrysavy, www.istockphoto.com

Figure 1.2. Sanjay C. Patel

Figure 1.3. Derived from janrysavy, www.istockphoto.com

Figure 1.4. Fig. 1, Millard F. Coffin, M.S. Pringle, R.A. Duncan, T.P. Gladczenko, M. Storey, R.D. Muller, and L.A. Gahagan, *Kerguelen Hotspot Magma Output since 130 Ma,* Journal of Petrology, Volume 43, Number 7, 2002, p. 1122.

Figure 2.1. Derived from *Reviews*, Paleozoic Fishes, Fig. 2, Dr. A. Fritsch, The Geological Magazine, Decade III, Volume VIII, Jan-Dec 1891, p. 376

Figure 2.2. Sanjay C. Patel

Figure 3.1. ESO/Y. Beletsky.

Figure 3.2. Volker Springel, Max-Planck-Institute for Astrophysics, Garching, Germany.

Figure 3.3. Marie Martig, Centre for Astrophysics and Supercomputing, Swinburne University of Technology, Hawthorn, Victoria 3122, Australia.

Figure 3.4. Sanjay C. Patel

Figure 3.5. Sanjay C. Patel

Figure 3.6. NASA, ESA, S. Beckwith (STScI), and The Hubble Heritage Team STScI/AURA.

Figure 3.7. ESA & NASA.

Figure 3.8. ESO

Figure 3.9. ESO

Figure 3.10. Derived from image by Andreas Koeberl, www.bigstockphoto.com

Figure 3.11. Derived from image by Buzlea Narcisa Floricica, www.istockphoto.com

Figure 3.12. Sanjay C. Patel

Figure 4.1. NASA, ESA, CXC, M. Bradac (University of California, Santa Barbara), and S. Allen (Stanford University).

Figure 4.2. Richard Powell, 'The Universe Within 1 Billion Light Years; The Neighbouring Superclusters.'

Figure 4.3. ESO

Figure 4.4. Sanjay C. Patel

Figure 4.5. Nataraja derived from Wildbird Images, www.istockphoto.com; The 'CfA2 Great Wall' from Ramella, Massimo; Geller, Margaret J.; Huchra, John P.; The two-point correlation function for groups of galaxies in the Center for Astrophysics redshift survey, Fig. 1a, Astrophysical Journal, Part 1 (ISSN 0004-637X), vol. 353, April 10, 1990, p. 52. DOI: 10.1086/168588

Figure 5.1. Derived from image by duncan1890, www.istockphoto.com

NOTES AND REFERENCES

1.　　Fabrice J. Fontaine, *A Si-Cl geothermobarometer for the reaction zone of high-temperature, basaltic-hosted mid-ocean ridge hydrothermal systems,* Volume 10, Number 5, 29 May 2009, Q05009, oi:10.1029/2009GC002407, Geochemistry, Geophysics, Geosystems, p. 3. Retrieved 29 June 2010; Fabrice J. Fontaine and William S. D. Wilcock, *Dynamics and storage of brine in mid-ocean ridge hydrothermal systems,* Journal of Geophysical Research, Vol. 111, B06102, 16 June 2006, p. 1. Retrieved 15 June 2008. http://www.agu.org/pubs/crossref/2006/2005JB003866.shtml

2.　　Dr. J.J. Rawal, Former Director: Nehru Planetarium, Mumbai, India; President: The Indian Planetary Society, Fellow: Gujarat Academy of Sciences; Member: The National Science Academy, India. Also, Professor Pankaj S. Joshi, Department of Astronomy and Astrophysics, Tata Institute of Fundamental Research, Homi Bhabha Road, Colaba, Mumbai 400005, India.

3.　　Sanjay C. Patel, *Deep-Sea Volcanoes and Their Associated Hydrothermal Vents,* Historical Notes, Indian National Science Academy (INSA), New Delhi, December 2004, 39.4 (2004), pp. 511-518; Sanjay C. Patel, *Who Really Discovered Deep-Sea Volcanoes?* IMAREST, Marine Scientist, No. 9, 4Q, December 2004, pp. 27-29; Sanjay C. Patel, *Who Were the Earliest Scholars of Submarine Volcanoes and Their Submerged Hydrothermal Vents?* 22nd International Congress of History of Science, Book of Abstracts, Beijing 24-30 July 2005, p. 355.

4.　　Fritjof Capra, *The Tao of Physics,* Shambhala (1991), p. 198

5.　　Carl Sagan, 1980, *Cosmos,* New York, Random House, p. 213-214

6.　　Ian Shaw, "Ancient History, Egyptians, 'Building the Great Pyramid,' Aligning," BBC Home, 2002-10-28. Retrieved 14 January 2008. http://www.bbc.co.uk/history/ancient/egyptians/great_pyramid_03.shtml

7.　　Tom M. Apostol, "The Tunnel of Samos," California Institute of Technology, *Engineering & Science*, No. 1, 2004, pp. 30-40. Retrieved 14 January 2008. http://eands.caltech.edu/articles/LXVII1/Apostol%20Feature%20(Samos).pdf

8.　　United Nations, UNESCO, Communication and Information, World Heritage, "Dholavira: a Harappan City, Gujarat, Disstt, Kachchh." Retrieved 7 August, 2008. http://whc.unesco.org/en/tentativelists/1090/ Also: Archaeological Survey of India, "Excavations - Dholavira, Dholavira." Retrieved 7 August 2008.

http://asi.nic.in/asi_exca_2007_dholavira.asp; BBC, "The Indians - What the Ancients Did For Us," bbc.co.uk/history, Video 2/6, BBC 4, 2006. Retrieved 27 November 2011. http://www.youtube.com/watch?v=dnlWvqQ-EtQ

9.   BBC, "The Indians - What the Ancients Did For Us," bbc.co.uk/history, Video 4/6, BBC 4, 2006. Retrieved 27 November 2011. http://www.youtube.com/watch?v=sVpLlz9SxlY; J.D. Verhoeven, A.H. Pendray, and W.E. Dauksch, The Key Role of Impurities in Ancient Damascus Steel Blades, Archaeotechnology, JOM, 50 (9) (1998), pp. 58-64; S. Srinivasan and S. Ranganathan, Wootz Steel: An Advanced Material of the Ancient World, Department of Metallurgy, Indian Institute of Science Bangalore. Retrieved 14 October 2011. http://www.tf.uni-kiel.de/matwis/amat/def_en/articles/wootz_advanced_material/wootz_steel.html

10.   BBC, "The Indians - What the Ancients Did For Us," bbc.co.uk/history, Video 5-6/6, BBC 4, 2006. Retrieved 27 November 2011. http://www.youtube.com/watch?v=k70TXn-H5Vo

11.   *Ibid.* Also R.E Rana and B.S Aror, "History of plastic surgery in India," Looking Back, The Journal of Postgraduate Medicine, Volume 48, Issue 1, 2002, pp. 76-8.

12.   National Geographic: *Moment of Death,* Peter Coyote, Documentary, Original Air Date: 2 September 2008.

13.   Carl Sagan, Cosmos: A Personal Voyage, Episode 12, Encyclopædia Galactica, PBS, 1980

14.   In some cases, passages of scripture that concern laws and customs may have been modified or interpolated at later dates from the original composition to evolve with emergencies, changing times, and needs. But passages on cosmology did not need to evolve and are therefore the most ancient. *The Book of Legends, Sefer Ha-Aggadah, Legends from the Talmud and Midrash,* Edited by Hayim Nahman Bialik and Yehoshua Hana Ravnitzky, translated by William G. Braude, Schoken Books, New York, 1992, p. xix

15.   Like the scientific figures themselves, these numerical convergences are usually accurate within 1-10 percent.

16.   Daniel C. Dennett, *Darwin's Dangerous Idea: Evolution and the Meanings of Life,* p. 28.

17.   Richard Dawkins, *The God Delusion*, Houghton Mifflin Company, 2006, pp. 111-151.

18.   Stephen Hawking, on Larry King Live, CNN, 9-10-2010, http://www.youtube.com/watch?v=9AdKEHzmqxA. Retrieved 27 November 2011.

19.   These metaphors are sometimes partially explained. For instance, the *Vishnu Purana*, which describes the movement of the Sun's 'chariot,'

drawn by seven horses along a wheel of three naves and five spokes. The passage says that the wheel is the perpetual 'wheel of time.' The three naves are the three times of day – dawn, noon, and dusk. The five spokes are a cyclical period of 5 years (known as a yuga) used for various mystical rituals. And the seven horses are the seven musical meters of the ancient scriptural passages. The chapter extends the metaphor and describes the various axles of the chariot, various poles, yokes and mountains along the wheel of time with the Pole star at its center. *Vishnu Purana*, translated by H.H. Wilson, edited by N.S. Singh, Nag Publishers: Delhi, 2003, Book II, Chpt VIII, vs. 2-7, footnote 3, p. 314. The five-year yuga speaks of the seasons. It seems not a cosmic period.

20.   UNESCO, *The Tradition of Vedic Chanting, INDIA,* Masterpieces of the Oral and Intangible Heritage of Humanity Proclamations 2001, 2003 and 2005, p. 46, http://unesdoc.unesco.org/images/0014/001473/147344e.pdf. Retrieved Nov 10, 2011

21.   Edwin Bryant, The Quest for the Origins of Vedic Culture: The Indo-Aryan Migration Debate, Oxford University Press, USA, March 11, 2004, p. 264-265

22.   Derived from the *Srimad Bhagavad Gita,* English translation and commentary by Swami Swarupananda, 1909.

23.   Derived from *The Upanishads,* Part 2, Sacred Books of the East, 15, translated by Max Müller, 1879.

24.   Daryl J. Bem, *Feeling the Future: Experimental Evidence for Anomalous Retroactive Influences on Cognition and Affect,* Journal of Personality and Social Psychology, Vol 100(3), Mar 2011, 407-425. doi: 10.1037/a0021524; Benedict Carey, *Journal's Paper on ESP Expected to Prompt Outrage,* The New York Times, January 5, 2011, http://www.nytimes.com/2011/01/06/science/06esp.html?pagewanted=all. Retrieved October 11, 2011

25.   *Bhagavad Gita,* 15.7, English translation and commentary by Swami Swarupananda, 1909.

26.   *Taittiriya Upanishad,* 2:9, *The Upanishads,* Part 2, Sacred Books of the East, 15, translated by Max Müller, 1879.

27.   *The Pew Forum on Religion and Public Life,* U.S. Religious Landscape Survey Resources, June 23 2008; David Van Biema, *Christians: No One Path to Salvation,* TIME, Monday, June 23, 2008, http://www.time.com/time/nation/article/0,8599,1817217,00.html#ixzz1OLkiHkIy

28.   Edward J. Larson and Larry Witham, *Scientists Are Still Keeping the Faith,* Nature, 386, 03 April 1997, pp. 435-436; doi:10.1038/386435a0

29.   *God Of The Quantum Vacuum,* New Scientist, volume 156, issue 2102, 4 Oct 1997, p. 28.

30.   This estimate derives from my survey of the literature.

31.   Peter Watson, *Ideas*, New York, NY: HarperCollins Publishers, p. 287

32.   The Meru has also been described as saucer shaped, braided and twisted, and octangular. (*Vayu Puranam,* 34:62-64) These are not contradictory descriptions, but the same pericarp viewed from various angles, ignoring or including its minute botanical characteristics.

33.   Yoga Vasishta 3.24.63

34.   Peter Watson, *Ideas*, New York, NY: HarperCollins Publishers, p. 424

35.   or solar system. *Beyond Earth, Mapping the Universe,* Edited by David DeVorkin, National Geographic, 2002, p. 107

36.   See Acknowledgments.

37.   Michael D. Lemonick; Andrea Dorfman/San Leandro, Irene M. Kunii/ Tokyo, Alice Park/Woods Hole And Tala Skari/Paris, *The Ocean Floor: The Last Frontier,* TIME, Monday, Aug. 14, 1995; http://www.time.com/time/printout/0,8816,983295,00.html; retrieved 12 Sept, 2011

38.   Fabrice J. Fontaine, *A Si-Cl geothermobarometer for the reaction zone of high-temperature, basaltic-hosted mid-ocean ridge hydrothermal systems,* Volume 10, Number 5, 29 May 2009, Q05009, oi:10.1029/2009GC002407, Geochemistry, Geophysics, Geosystems, p. 3. Retrieved 29 June 2010; Fabrice J. Fontaine and William S. D. Wilcock, *Dynamics and storage of brine in mid-ocean ridge hydrothermal systems,* Journal of Geophysical Research, Vol. 111, B06102, 16 June 2006, p. 1. Retrieved 15 June 2008. http://www.agu.org/pubs/crossref/2006/2005JB003866.shtml

39.   Fisher, A.T., Urabe, T., Klaus, A., and the Expedition 301 Scientists, *Expedition 301 synthesis: hydrogeologic studies,* Proceedings of the Integrated Ocean Drilling Program, Volume 301, doi:10.2204/iodp.proc.301.206.2009, p. 1, 3.

40.   *Hydrothermal Vents,* Science Encyclopedia Vol. 3, http://science.jrank.org/pages/3476/Hydrothermal-Vents.html. Retrieved 27 November 2011.

41.   *Underwater Gold,* New Scientist, 128, Issue 1743 (1990); National Oceanic And and Atmospheric Administration, *Vent Geochemistry: Circulation Zones.* http://www.pmel.noaa.gov/vents/chemistry/circulation.html. Retrieved 10 September 10, 2003.

42.   *Explosive volcanism on the ultraslow-spreading Gakkel ridge,* Arctic Ocean, Letter, Nature 453, pp. 1236-1238, 26 June 2008; http://www.nature.com/nature/journal/v453/n7199/abs/nature07075.html ; Hillary Mayell, *Scientists Excited By Arctic Ocean Ridge Finds,* National Geographic News, November 29, 2001. http://news.nationalgeographic.com/news/2001/11/1129_icebreaker.html

; *More deep-sea vents discovered,* National Oceanography Centre, Southampton (UK), February 14, 2011. Retrieved 5 June 2011, http://noc.ac.uk/news/more-deep-sea-vents-discovered

43. Jyotiranjan S. Ray, S. K. Pattanayak, and Kanchan Pande, *Rapid emplacement of the Kerguelen plume–related Sylhet Traps, eastern India: Evidence from 40Ar-39Ar geochronology,* abstract, Geophysical Research Letters, vol. 32, 20 May 2005. L10303, doi:10.1029/2005GL022586, 2005. http://www.agu.org/pubs/crossref/2005/2005GL022586.shtml.

44. Millard F. Coffin, M.S. Pringle, R.A. Duncan, T.P. Gladczenko, M. Storey, R.D. Muller, and L.A. Gahagan, *Kerguelen Hotspot Magma Output since 130 Ma,* Journal of Petrology, Volume 43, Number 7, 2002, p. 1126.

45. *UT Austin scientist plays major role in study of underwater 'microcontinent,'* News, The University of Texas, 28 May 28, 1999. http://www.utexas.edu/news/1999/05/28/nr_continent/. Retrieved 27 November 2011.

46. *Eruption Environment and Impact, Ocean Drilling Program (ODP),* Texas A&M University, College of Geosciences, http://www-odp.tamu.edu/publications/183_SR/synth/synth_7.htm. Retrieved 27 November 2011.

47. Barbara A.R. Mohr, Veronika Wähnert, and David Lazarus, *Mid-Cretaceous Paleobotany and Palynology of the Central Kerguelen Plateau,* Southern Indian Ocean (ODP Leg 183, Site 1138), Ocean Drilling Program (ODP), Abstract, 3, Texas A&M University, College of Geosciences, 13 September 2002; *UT Austin scientist plays major role in study of underwater 'micro-continent,'* News, The University of Texas, 28 May 28, 1999. http://www.utexas.edu/news/1999/05/28/nr_continent/. Retrieved 27 November 2011.

48. *Eruption Environment and Impact,* Ocean Drilling Program (ODP), Texas A&M University, College of Geosciences, http://www-odp.tamu.edu/publications/183_SR/synth/synth_7.htm. Retrieved 27 November 2011.

49. Brian Handwerk, *Hydrothermal "Megaplume" Found in Indian Ocean,* National Geographic News, 12 December 12, 2005. http://news.nationalgeographic.com/news/2005/12/1212_051212_mega plume.html. Retrieved 27 November 2011.

50. Some texts say Vishnu or others. Brahma is a deity that presides over a unit of the universe called a Brahmanda or cosmic egg. There are many such eggs and Brahmas. There are three frequently used terms in Yoga Literature that are similar in spelling and therefore commonly confused: 'Brahma,' 'Brahman,' and 'Brahmin.' The meanings of these three terms are very distinct. Brahmin refers to a human being of the Hindu priestly order. Brahman refers to the enlightened Soul-Self, and in some con-

texts, to God or his abode. Brahma refers to a heavenly being responsible for the structuring of one brahmanda (or galaxy) and the creation of its life forms. There are therefore as many Brahmas as there are galaxies.

51. There are other versions of the story.

52. *Vishnu Purana*, translated by H.H. Wilson, edited by N.S. Singh, Nag Publishers: Delhi, 2003, Book I, Chpt III, vs. 10-16, Commentary, pp. 34-35; Shri Swaminarayan, Vachanamruta, Bhugol Khagol, Swaminarayan Aksharpith, English Translation, 2006, p. 700

53. *Vishnu Purana*, translated by H.H. Wilson, edited by N.S. Singh, Nag Publishers: Delhi, 2003, Book I, Chpt III, vs. 10-16, Commentary, pp. 34-35.

54. Peter D. Ward and Donald Brownlee, *The Life and Death of Planet Earth,* Owl Books, 2003, p. 30-31, 147

55. Nicolas Flamenta, Nicolas Colticea, and Patrice F. Reyb, *A case for late-Archaean continental emergence from thermal evolution models and hypsometry,* Earth and Planetary Science Letters, Volume 275, Issues 3-4, 15 November 2008, pp. 326-336

56. N.J. Vlaar, *Continental Emergence And Growth On A Cooling Earth,* Tectonophysics 322, 2000, 191-202; also Seno, T & Honda, S., *Mantle Convection And Global Sea Level: Implications For The Environmental Evolution,* AGU, 1999 AGU Fall Meeting. http://www.agu.org/meetings/waisfm99.html; N. Flament, N. Coltice, and P. Rey, *Emerged land surface in the Archean: constraints on continental growth and mantle thermal history,* European Geosciences Union 2007, Geophysical Research Abstracts, Vol. 9, 06647, 2007.

57. *Prehistoric Time Line,* National Geographic.com, Devonian Period, http://science.nationalgeographic.com/science/prehistoric-world/devonian/

58. Derived from *Reviews*, Paleozoic Fishes, Fig. 2, Dr. A. Fritsch, The Geological Magazine, Decade III, Volume VIII, Jan-Dec 1891, p. 376

59. *'Link' Between Fish and Land Animals Found,* Guy Gugliotta, Washington Post, April 6, 2006. http://www.washingtonpost.com/wp-dyn/content/article/2006/04/05/AR2006040502369_pf.html

60. *Climate Change,* The Palaeobiology and Biodiversity Research Group (PBRG), Dept. of Earth Sciences, University of Bristol. Retrieved June 5, 2011, http://palaeo.gly.bris.ac.uk/Palaeofiles/Permian/climate.html

61. Douglas H. Erwin, *Extinction*, Princeton University Press, 2006, Cover, Inner Flap; Rosalind V. White, *Earth's biggest 'whodunnit': unravelling the clues in the case of the end-Permian mass extinction,* Philosophical Transactions of the Royal Society A (2002) 360, 2963–2, 24 October

2002,
http://rsta.royalsocietypublishing.org/content/360/1801/2963.full.pdf

62. Douglas H. Erwin, *Extinction*, Princeton University Press, 2006, p. 194

63. *Ibid.*, p. 14.

64. Mauro Rosi, Paolo Papale, Luca Lupi, and Marco Stoppato, "Volca-noes" (a Firefly Guide), p. 30, 40, 2003.

65. Douglas H. Erwin, *Extinction*, Princeton University Press, 2006, p. 192.

66. Powers, C.M. and D.J. Bottjer. 2007. Bryozoan paleoecology indicates mid-Phanerozoic extinctions were the product of long-term environmental stress. Geology, 35: 995-998.

67. Anthony Hallam, *Phanerozoic Sea-Level Changes,* Columbia University Press, 1992, p. 81; Harries P. J., *Epeiric Seas: A Continental Extension of Shelf Biotas,* Earth System: History and Natuaral Viability, Vol. 1, Encyclopedia of Life Support Systems (EOLSS), UNESCO, Eolss Publishers Co. Ltd, Figure 1, p. 4; Douglas H. Erwin, *Extinction*, Princeton University Press, 2006, p. 189, 176.

68. Anthony Hallam, *Phanerozoic Sea-Level Changes,* Columbia University Press, 1992, p. 83, 86-87; Douglas H. Erwin, *Extinction*, Princeton University Press, 2006, p. 176.

69. Harries P. J., *Epeiric Seas: A Continental Extension of Shelf Biotas,* Earth System: History and Natuaral Viability, Vol. 1, Encyclopedia of Life Support Systems (EOLSS), UNESCO, Eolss Publishers Co. Ltd, p. 2.

70. Douglas H. Erwin, *Extinction*, Princeton University Press, 2006, p. 7.

71. *Ibid.*, p. 26.

72. Cuppone, Tiberio, Camp Volcanism: age, volcanic stratigraphy and origin of the magmas. Cases studies from Morocco and the U.S.A., Padua@research, 2009

73. Douglas H. Erwin, *Extinction*, Princeton University Press, 2006, p. 26.

74. Anthony Hallam, *Phanerozoic Sea-Level Changes,* Columbia University Press, 1992, Figure 4.1, p. 90-91; David E. Fastovsky and David B. Weishampel, *The Evolution and Extinction of the Dinosaurs,* Cambridge University Press (1996), p. 32.

75. Bilal U. Haq, Jan Hardenbol, Peter R. Vail, *Chronology of Fluctuating Sea Levels Since the Triassic,* www.sciencemag.org on October 28, 2008; retrieved from http://www.mantleplumes.org/WebDocuments/Haq1987.pdf, June 21 2011, p. 1163; Tom McCann, *The Geology of Central Europe: Mesozoic and Cenozoic,* Vol. 2, Geological Society of London, 2008, p. 832

76. Andy Coghlan, *One world, 8.7 million species, most still unknown,* New Scientist,

http://www.newscientist.com/article/dn20825-one-world-87-million-spe cies-most-still-unknown.html, 24 August 2011. Retrieved Sept 4 2011

77. Camilo Mora, Derek P. Tittensor, Sina Adl, Alastair G. B. Simpson, Boris Worm, *How Many Species Are There on Earth and in the Ocean?* PLoS Biol 9(8): e1001127. doi:10.1371/journal.pbio.1001127, August 23, 2011

78. Peter D. Ward and Donald Brownlee, *The Life and Death of Planet Earth,* Owl Books, 2003, p. 30-31, 147; Nicolas Flamenta, Nicolas Colticea, and Patrice F. Reyb, *A case for late-Archaean continental emergence from thermal evolution models and hypsometry,* Earth and Planetary Science Letters, Volume 275, Issues 3-4, 15 November 2008, pp. 326-336 doi:10.1016/j.epsl.2008.08.029, http://www.earthbyte.org/people/dietmar/Pdf/Flament_etal_case_for_arc haean_continental_emergence.pdf

79. *The First Life on Earth, The Archean, Geologic Time,* Smithsonian National Museum of Natural History, Retrieved No 10, 2011, http://paleobiology.si.edu/geotime/main/htmlversion/archean3.html

80. NASA News Release, *NASA Research Indicates Oxygen on Earth 2.5 Billion Years Ago,* Sept. 27, 2007, http://www.nasa.gov/centers/ames/news/releases/2007/07_70AR.html. Retrieved Nov 10, 2011; *Prehistoric Time Line,* National Geographic.com, http://science.nationalgeographic.com/science/prehistoric-world/prehisto ric-time-line.html

81. David Lambert and the Diagram Group, *The Field Guide to Geology,* Checkmark Books, 2007, p. 190-191; *Prehistoric Time Line,* National Geographic.com, http://science.nationalgeographic.com/science/prehistoric-world/prehisto ric-time-line.html

82. *Prehistoric Time Line,* National Geographic.com, http://science.nationalgeographic.com/science/prehistoric-world/prehisto ric-time-line.html

83. *Ibid.*

84. David Lambert and the Diagram Group, *The Field Guide to Geology,* Checkmark Books, 2007, p. 205; *Prehistoric Time Line,* National Geographic.com, http://science.nationalgeographic.com/science/prehistoric-world/prehisto ric-time-line.html

85. *Prehistoric Time Line,* National Geographic.com, http://science.nationalgeographic.com/science/prehistoric-world/prehisto ric-time-line.html

86. F. Spoor, M. G. Leakey, P. N. Gathogo, F. H. Brown, S. C. Antón, I. McDougall, C. Kiarie, F. K. Manthi & L. N. Leakey, *Implications of*

new early Homo fossils from Ileret, east of Lake Turkana, Kenya, Nature 448 (448): 688–691, 9 August 2007, doi:10.1038/nature05986.

87. Derived from *The Mahabharata of Krishna-Dwaipayana Vyasa,* translated by Kisari Mohan Ganguli, published between 1883 and 1896, p. 858, http://www.sacred-texts.com/index.htm. Retrieved 17 August 2011.

88. The four modes: womb, egg, seed, and putrefaction. *Matsya Purana 1.29-32*

89. Derived from *The prologue to the Rámáyana of Tulsi Dás: a specimen translation By Tulasīdāsa,* Frederic Salmon Growse, from The Journal Asiatic Society of Bengal, Vol. XLV, Part 1, 1876, *Bk 1, Soratha 1, Doha 8-11, Chaupai* p. 9, (Google ebook); *Sri Ramacaritamanasa,* Gita Press, Gorakhpur, India, p. 32, http://www.gitapress.org/BOOKS/1318/1318_Sri%20Ramchritmanas_R oman.pdf - retrieved 7 Sept 2011

90. Marcia Bartusiak, *Archives of the Universe,* Pantheon Books, 2004, pp. 313-314, pp. 415-416; V.M. Slipher, *Spectrographic Observations of Nebulae,* Popular Astronomy 23, 1915, pp. 21-24.

91. Allan Sandage, *Edwin Hubble 1889-1953,* The Journal of the Royal Astronomical Society of Canada, Vol. 83, No.6, December 1989, Whole No. 621, p. 357, http://apod.nasa.gov/diamond_jubilee/1996/sandage_hubble.html; Hubble, E. 1953, Mon. Not. Roy. Astron. Soc., 113, 658; Marcia Bartusiak, *Archives of the Universe,* Pantheon Books, 2004, p. 417

92. Steven Weinberg, *Cosmology,* Oxford University Press, 2008, p. 44

93. Marcia Bartusiak, *Archives of the Universe,* Pantheon Books, 2004, p. 314

94. Georges Lemaître, *Un Univers homogène de masse constante et de rayon croissant rendant compte de la vitesse radiale des nébuleuses extra-galactiques,* Annales de la Société Scientifique de Bruxelles, Vol. 47, p. 49, April 1927; Abbe Georges Lemaitre, *A Homogenous Universe of Constant Mass and Increasing Radius Accounting for the Radial Velocity of Extra-Galactic Nebulae,* Monthly Notices of the Royal Astronomical Society, vol. 91, March 1931; Marcia Bartusiak, *Archives of the Universe,* Pantheon Books, 2004, p. 314

95. Marcia Bartusiak, *Archives of the Universe,* Pantheon Books, 2004, p. 321

96. Georges Lemaitre, quoted in *New York Times Magazine,* February 19, 1933.

97. NASA, Wilkinson Microwave Anisotropy Probe, *Cosmology: The Study of the Universe,* http://map.gsfc.nasa.gov/universe/WMAP_Universe.pdf. Retrieved June 21 2011, p. 10

98. Richard B. Larson and Volker Bromm, *The First Stars in the Universe,* Scientific American, December 2001; p. 6

99. Bradley W. Carroll and Dale A. Ostlie, *An Introduction to Modern Astrophysics,* Addison-Wesley, 2007, p. 1256; *How Old Is The Milky Way? VLT Observations Of Beryllium In Two Old Stars Clock The Beginnings,* European Space Organisation (ESO) Press Release 20/04, 17 August 2004. http://www.eso.org/outreach/press-rel/pr-2004/pr-20-04.html

100. Bradley W. Carroll and Dale A. Ostlie, *An Introduction to Modern Astrophysics,* Addison-Wesley, 2007, Table 24.1, p. 884, p. 894-895; L. Origlia, Lena, E. Diolaiti, F. R. Ferraro, E. Valenti, S. Fabbri, and G. Beccari, *Probing the Galactic Bulge with Deep Adaptive Optics imaging: the Age of NGC 64401,* The Astrophysical Journal, 687: L79–L82, 2008 November 10, p. L82; Manuela Zoccali, Vanessa Hill, Beatriz Barbuy, Aurelie Lecureur, Dante Minniti, Alvio Renzini, Oscar Gonzalez1, Ana Gómez, Sergio Ortolani, *Chemistry of the Galactic Bulge: New Results,* Astronomical Science, The Messenger 136, June 2009, p. 53; Cristina Chiappini, *The Formation and Evolution of the Milky Way,* American Scientist, the magazine of Sigma Xi, The Scientific Research Society, 2001, p. 5.

101. Peter D. Ward and Donald Brownlee, *The Life and Death of Planet Earth,* Owl Books, 2003, p. 159

102. Bradley W. Carroll and Dale A. Ostlie, *An Introduction to Modern Astrophysics,* Addison-Wesley, 2007, Table 24.1, p. 884

103. Bradley W. Carroll and Dale A. Ostlie, *An Introduction to Modern Astrophysics,* Addison-Wesley, 2007, Table 24.1, p. 884; L. Origlia, Lena, E. Diolaiti, F. R. Ferraro, E. Valenti, S. Fabbri, and G. Beccari, *Probing the Galactic Bulge with Deep Adaptive Optics imaging: the Age of NGC 64401,* The Astrophysical Journal, 687: L79–L82, 2008 November 10, p. L82; Manuela Zoccali, Vanessa Hill, Beatriz Barbuy, Aurelie Lecureur, Dante Minniti, Alvio Renzini, Oscar Gonzalez1, Ana Gómez, Sergio Ortolani, *Chemistry of the Galactic Bulge: New Results,* Astronomical Science, The Messenger 136, June 2009, p. 53

104. April Kemick, *Supernovae Not What They Used To Be,* the Bulletin, University of Toronto, October 10, 2007, 61st year, number 5, p.7; D. Andrew Howell, Mark Sullivan, Alex Conley, Ray Carlberg, *Predicted and Observed Evolution in the Mean Properties of Type Ia Supernovae with Redshift,* arXiv:astro-ph/0701912v2 1 Aug 2007.

105. Jochen M. Braun, Dominik J. Bomans, Jean-Marie Will, and Klaas S. de Boer, *No stellar age gradient inside supergiant shell LMC4?,* Astronomy and Astrophysics, 328, 1997, pp. 167-174.

106. *The Milky Way has a double halo,* News Release, Sloan Digital Sky Survey, December 12, 2007, http://www.sdss.org/news/releases/20071212.dblhalo.html.

107. *New Milky Way Map Reveals a Complicated Outer Galaxy,* Sloan Digital Sky Survey, Mapping the Universe, August 16, 2008, http://www.sdss.org/news/releases/20080816.segue_final.html; *Show 182: Stellar Streams,* Hubblesite, Skywatch With Hubble Watch, http://hubblesite.org/explore_astronomy/skywatch/+19, mp3 audio. Retrieved Sept 21 2011

108. Bradley W. Carroll and Dale A. Ostlie, *An Introduction to Modern Astrophysics,* Addison-Wesley, 2007, p. 1025

109. C. M. Violette Impellizzeri, John P. McKean, Paola Castangia, Alan L. Roy, Christian Henkel, Andreas Brunthaler, & Olaf Wucknitz, *A gravitationally lensed water maser in the early Universe,* Nature 456, 927-929, 18 December 2008, | doi:10.1038/nature07544

110. Andrew Fazekas, Black Hole Hosts Universe's Most Massive Water Cloud, National Geographic News, July 27, 2011

111. J.P. McKean, C.M.V. Impellizzeri, A.L. Roy, P. Castangia, F. Samuel, A. Brunthaler, C. Henkel and O. Wucknitz, *A search for gravitationally lensed water masers in dusty quasars and star-forming galaxies,* Mon. Not. R. Astron. Soc. (2010), 2010 September 1. doi:10.1111/j.1365-2966.2010.17617.x; correspondence, Rich Barvainis, 11/11/10.

112. *NASA's Spitzer Space Telescope Exposes Dusty Galactic Hideouts,* Mission News, Mar. 1, 2005, http://www.nasa.gov/vision/universe/starsgalaxies/spitzer-030105.html; Peter Schneider, *Extragalactic Astronomy and Cosmology,* Springer, 2006, pp. 389-390.

113. *10,000 Earths' Worth of Fresh Dust Found Near Star Explosion,* NASA Newsroom, December 20, 2007, http://www.spitzer.caltech.edu/Media/releases/ssc2007-20/release.shtml; J. Rho, T. Kozasa, W. T. Reach, J. D. Smith, L. Rudnick, T. DeLaney, J. A. Ennis, H. Gomez, and A. Tappe, 2008, *Freshly Formed Dust in the Cassiopeia A Supernova Remnant as Revealed by the Spitzer Space Telescope,* The Astrophysical Journal 673:1, 271-282, Online publication date: 20-Jan-2008.

114. J. Guo, F. Zhang, X. Chen, and Z. Han, *Probability Distribution of Terrestrial Planets in Habitable Zones around Host Stars,* Astronomy & Astrophysics, March 9, 2010; C. Melis, B. Zuckerman, J. H. Rhee, I. Song, *The Age of the HD 15407 System and the Epoch of Final Catastrophic Mass Accretion onto Terrestrial Planets around Sun-like Stars,* arXiv:1005.2451v2 [astro-ph.SR] 17 May 2010

115. G. Schilling, *'Super-Earth' Found in Habitable Zone,* SCIENCENOW, 12 September 2011; M. R. Meyer, J. M. Carpenter, E. E. Mamajek, L. A. Hillenbrand, D. Hollenbach, A. Moro-Martin, J. S. Kim, M. D. Silverstone, J. Najita, D. C. Hines, I. Pascucci, J. R. Stauffer, J. Bouwman, and D. E. Backman, *Evolution of Mid-Infrared Excess*

around Sun-like Stars: Constraints on Models of Terrestrial Planet Formation, The Astrophysical Journal, 673:L181–L184, 2008 February 1, p. 7

116. Charles H. Lineweaver, *An Estimate of the Age Distribution of Terrestrial Planets in the Universe: Quantifying Metallicity as a Selection Effect,* Icarus, Volume 151, Issue 2, June 2001, pp. 307-313.

117. James B. Kaler, Professor Emeritus of Astronomy, University of Illinois, correspondence.

118. G. Schilling, *'Super-Earth' Found in Habitable Zone,* SCIENCENOW, 12 September 2011; *Planète Habitable, Des chercheurs découvrent une planète potentiellement habitable,* Info rédaction, publiée le 30 août 2011, http://www.maxisciences.com/plan%E8te-habitable/des-chercheurs-decouvrent-une-planete-potentiellement-habitable_art16635.html; Ivan Semeniuk, *Most Earth-like planet yet spotted in a habitable zone,* Nature.com, Newsblog, September 29, 2010; Mark Peplow, *Found: one Earth-like planet,* Nature, News, doi:10.1038/news060123-5, Published online 25 January 2006, http://blogs.nature.com/news/2010/09/most_earthlike_planet_yet_spot.html

119. Charles H. Lineweaver, Yeshe Fenner, and Brad K. Gibson, *The Galactic Habitable Zone and the Age Distribution of Complex Life in the Milky Way,* Science, Jan 2, 2004, http://arxiv.org/pdf/astro-ph/0401024; Charles H. Lineweaver and Tamara M. Davis, *Does the Rapid Appearance of Life on Earth Suggest that Life is Common in the Universe?* arXiv:astro-ph/0205014v2, 8 May 2003; I. S. Shklovskii and Carl Sagan, *Intelligent Life in the Universe,* Emerson-Adams Press, 1 edition, November 16, 1998

120. Bradley W. Carroll and Dale A. Ostlie, *An Introduction to Modern Astrophysics,* Addison-Wesley, 2007, Table 24.1, p. 884

121. Cristina Chiappini, *The Formation and Evolution of the Milky Way,* American Scientist, the magazine of Sigma Xi, The Scientific Research Society, 2001, p. 9-10; Chris Brook, Vincent Veilleux, Daisuke Kawata, Hugo Martell, Brad Gibson, *Gas Rich Mergers in Disk Formation,* arXiv: astro-ph/0511002v1, 31 Oct 2005; Tetyana V. Nykytyuk And Tamara V. Mishenina, *The Galactic Thick And Thin Disks: Differences In Evolution,* Astronomy & Astrophysics, European Space Organisation (ESO), May 21, 2006, arXiv:astro-ph/0605661v1.

122. Bradley W. Carroll and Dale A. Ostlie, *An Introduction to Modern Astrophysics,* Addison-Wesley, 2007, Table 24.1, p. 884, 886; M. Haywood, *The transition between the thick and thin Galactic disks, A Giant Step: from Milli- to Micro-arcsecond Astrometry,* Proceedings IAU Symposium No. 248, 2007, International Astronomical Union, doi:10.1017/S1743921308019807, p. 461; Feltzing, S.,Bensby, T.,&

Lundstrom, I. 2003, Astronomy & Astrophysics, 397, 1L quoted in Tetyana V. Nykytyuk And Tamara V. Mishenina, *The Galactic Thick And Thin Disks: Differences In Evolution,* Astronomy & Astrophysics, European Space Organisation (ESO), May 21, 2006, arXiv:astro-ph/0605661v1. p. 1.

123. Brian Abbott, *The Milky Way Atlas, The Digital Universe Guide,* for Partiview, Hayden Planetarium, American Museum of Natural History, New York, NY USA, http://haydenplanetarium.org/universe/ December 19, 2007, p. 24

124. *Ibid.*

125. James B. Kaler, *Cambridge Encyclopedia of Stars,* Cambridge University Press, 2006, p. 80

126. R. Launhardt, R. Zylka, and P.G. Mezger, *The nuclear bulge of the Galaxy. III. Large-scale physical characteristics of stars and interstellar matter,* Astronomy & Astrophysics 384, 112-139 (2002), DOI: 10.1051/0004-6361:20020017

127. Bradley W. Carroll and Dale A. Ostlie, *An Introduction to Modern Astrophysics,* Addison-Wesley, 2007, p. 923

128. Fred Adams and Greg Laughlin, *The Five Ages of the Universe,* Touchstone, 1999, p. 72.

129. Robert A. Oden, *Cosmogony, Cosmology,* in vol. 1 of ABD, ed. D. N. Freedman, New York: Doubleday, 1992, pp. 1162-71

130. Interestingly, the pre-eminent Yogi also states that "At the time of dissolution, the 'disk of earth' will again be in the form of a fundamental particle." He does not state when this time will be, however, scientists have proposed a similar cyclic model. Paul J. Steinhardt and Neil Turok, *Cyclic Model of the Universe,* Originally published in Science Express on 25 April 2002, Science 24 May 2002, Vol. 296. no. 5572, pp. 1436-1439; Paul Steinhardt, *Cyclic Universe – Does the universe repeat once every trillion years?* Incubator, Seed, SeedMagazine.com, Posted July 2, 2007. http://seedmagazine.com/news/2007/07/a_cyclic_universe.php?page=all &p=y; Martin Bojowald, *Big Bang or Big Bounce?* Scientific American, October 6, 2008.

131. Shri Swaminarayan, *Vedras,* Bochasanwasi Shri Akshar Purushottam Sanstha, 1978, p. 91.

132. Derived from image by Andreas Koeberl, Stock Photo: 22512953, www.bigstockphoto.com, Retrieved 25 Sep 2011

133. *Vishnu Purana,* translated by H.H. Wilson, edited by N.S. Singh, Nag Publishers: Delhi, 2003, Book II, Chpt VIII, vs. 20, Footnote 8, p. 317

134. *Bhagavata Purana,* 2.9.1-45; 2.10.1-47; 3.8.1-33; 3.9.1-43; 3.10.1-29

135. *Ibid.,* 2.6.41

136. This unnamed kalpa is sometimes erroneously referred to as the Brahma Kalpa. The Brahma Kalpa, however, refers to the very first day of Brahma's 100 year lifespan. "At the beginning of the first half of Brahma's life, was the great Brahma Kalpa, when Brahma appeared along with the sound of the Vedas or the word 'Brahm.' (Bhagavata Purana, 3.11.35-37) It's a very holy kalpa being the day on which the cosmic being Purusha (also called Virat or Vairaj Purusha) announced the first holy word "Brahm" as well as the Vedas. The Vedas were taught to Brahma who also recited it. (Bhagavata Purana, 3.4.13) Brahma's entire lifespan of 100 years is equivalent to about 311 trillion human years. It's divided into two halves called 'Parardhas.' The First Parardha of Brahma's life, beginning with the celebrated Brahma Kalpa, is already over. It ended with the Padma Kalpa. Currently, we're moving towards the end of the first kalpa named the Varaha of the second Parardha of his life. (Markandeya Puranam, 43:43-44) The unnamed kalpa previous to the Padma shouldn't be identified with the first momentous Brahma Kalpa for the following overwhelming reason: the narrative of creation describes the last three kalpas as *consecutive.* That means the Yogis have only narrated the history of Brahma's last three days. We have little idea of what transpired across his previous 50 year lifespan.

137. Bradley W. Carroll and Dale A. Ostlie, *An Introduction to Modern Astrophysics,* Addison-Wesley, 2007, p. 1058, 1069; The High Energy Astrophysics Science Archive Research Center (HEASARC), NASA, *The Nearest Superclusters,* http://heasarc.nasa.gov/docs/cosmic/nearest_superclusters_info.html; Compact Objects at Wisconsin (COW), the University of Wisconsin-Madison, Departments of Physics and Astronomy, and Madison Area Science and Technology (MAST), *The Great Attractor,* http://cow.physics.wisc.edu/~ogelman/guide/gr8a/; Galaxy Distribution, http://www.tufts.edu/as/wright_center/cosmic_evolution/docs/text/text_gal_2.html; retrieved 15 Sept 2011

138. *The Universe Within 1 Billion Light Years, The Neighbouring Superclusters,* http://www.atlasoftheuniverse.com/superc.html. Retrieved 25 Sept 2011

139. Elena D'Onghia, Gurtina Besla, Thomas J. Cox, Lars Hernquist, *Resonant stripping as the origin of dwarf spheroidal galaxies,* Nature 460, Letter, 30 July 2009, pp. 605-607 doi:10.1038/nature08215

140. Donna Weaver and Michael Corbin, *A Tiny Galaxy is Born,* Hubblesite, News Release Number: STScI-2002-16, December 19, 2002, http://hubblesite.org/newscenter/archive/releases/2002/16/ Retrieved 27 November 2011.

141. Friedrich Otto Schrader, *Introduction to the Pancaratra and Ahirbudhnya Samhita,* 1916, p. 81.

NOTES AND REFERENCES

142. Sharada Srinivasana, *Shiva as 'cosmic dancer': On Pallava origins for the Nataraja bronze,* World Archaeology, Volume 36, Issue 3, 2004, DOI:10.1080/1468936042000282726821, p. 433

143. Sharada Srinivasana, *Shiva as 'cosmic dancer': On Pallava origins for the Nataraja bronze,* World Archaeology, Volume 36, Issue 3, 2004, DOI:10.1080/1468936042000282726821, p. 433

144. Klaus K. Klostermaier, *A Survey of Hinduism,* Suny Press, 2007, p. 109-111

145. The 'CfA2 Great Wall' from the article: Ramella, Massimo; Geller, Margaret J.; Huchra, John P., *The two-point correlation function for groups of galaxies in the Center for Astrophysics redshift survey,* Fig. 1a, Astrophysical Journal, Part 1 (ISSN 0004-637X), vol. 353, April 10, 1990, p. 52. DOI: 10.1086/168588

146. Sharada Srinivasan, *Cosmic Dance*, India International Centre (IIC) Quarterly, Autumn 2007, p. 129.

147. This round number is quite by accident. There are many more correspondences to be found in other subjects to be covered in my next book. See www.SanjayPatel.co for more details.

148. Genesis 1.

149. *Bible,* Genesis 15:12, 17; 19:23; and 37:9.

150. This figure does not conflict with the Yogis' longer unit of 4.32 billion years. The Israelites were using a similar system as the Yogis, only with a smaller calibration. There is no essential difference between the Yogis' method of calibrating astronomical periods of time and those used in the Bible just as there is no essential difference between measuring distances in kilometers or miles. It's merely a question of convention, culture, or personal preference. In the Biblical tradition, the ancient teachers used a smaller unit that equalled about half the Yogic unit.

151. Creation progresses chronologically as Brahma utters their names. As such, to create the three worlds, he states 'bhuh-bhuvah-svah' or 'earth-firmament-heaven' in this order. (*Bhagavata Purana* 3.9 and 3.10)

152. Though the early galaxy was lit by supernovae, its stars did not live long and did not form a permanent structure like the halo stars, bulge, and Sun. Genesis describes only the permanent structures of the Galaxy.

153. *Bible,* Genesis 1, 1:6-1:8, Hebrew Interlinear Bible (OT), http://www.scripture4all.org/OnlineInterlinear/OTpdf/gen1.pdf. Retrieved 27 November 2011; H. F. W. Gesenius, Francis Brown, Edward Robinson, S. R. Driver, Charles A. Briggs, *The Old Testament Hebrew Lexicon*, http://www.biblestudytools.net/Lexicons/Hebrew/ Retrieved 27 November 2011.

154. The thick and thin disks as a whole. Bradley W. Carroll and Dale A. Ostlie, *An Introduction to Modern Astrophysics,* Addison-Wesley, 2007, Table 24.1, p. 884

155. *Vishnu Purana*, 2.7.16

156. James B. Kaler, Professor Emeritus of Astronomy, University of Illinois, correspondence.

157. You may also note that there is a common characteristic in each of the cosmic structures described: they are all permanent (or long-term) structures. Genesis 1, like the Yoga Literature, not only bequeaths an abstraction of cosmic creation, but exclusively describes only the permanent features of our Galaxy that are still tangible today, not the transitory ones of the past.

158. There have been some scientific studies suggesting the universe may be about 1 billion years older than believed, making it about 14.7 billion years old. (David L Wiltshire *Cosmic clocks, cosmic variance and cosmic averages,* 2007, New J. Phys. 9 377, 22 October 2007; Ben M. Leith, S. C. Cindy Ng, and David L. Wiltshire, *Gravitational Energy as Dark Energy: Concordance of Cosmological Tests,* The Astrophysical Journal, 672:L91–L94, 2008 January 10.) Would the timeframe given by the Puranas or Genesis be affected if the universe is taken to be 14.7 billion years old? No. The timeframe hardly changes at all. It would lead to an increase in the length of each Biblical day from 2.283 billion years to about 2.45 billion years, which is a difference of about 7%. You need to remember that even the scientific figures are only approximations themselves. And so are the descriptions in ancient scripture.

159. See upcoming second book for 10 more convergences on this topic and many others or visit www.SanjayPatel.co.

160. Fred Adams and Greg Laughlin, *The Five Ages of the Universe,* Touchstone, 1999, p. 47, 50.

161. Peter D. Ward and Donald Brownlee, *The Life and Death of Planet Earth,* Owl Books, 2003, p. 149

162. K.P. Schroder and Robert Connon Smith, *Distant future of the Sun and Earth revisited,* Mon. Not. R. Astron. Soc. 000, 1–10, 2008, 3 February 2008, p. 7

163. *Ibid.*, p. 3

164. It's a vision of the future, the day of God. The original quote says: "The devil who deceived them was thrown into the lake of fire and sulfur." *World English Bible*, public domain, http://ebible.org/web/

165. The metaphorical nature of the ancient Vedas has been acknowledged by H.H. Wilson, *Vishnu Puranam*, edited by N.S. Singh, Nag Publishers: Delhi, 2003, Book II, Chpt XI, vs. 11, footnote 1, p. 340.

166. The words *bhumi, antariksha,* and *dyau* are synonymous with the popular *bhuh, bhuvah, svah* respectively or *bhur loka, bhuvar loka,* and *swarga loka.*

167. Derived from *Rig Veda Samhita*, translation according to Wilson, H.H. & Bhashya of Sayanacharya, edited by Arya, R.P. & Joshi, K.L., Parimal Publications: Delhi, 2005.

168. Oral tradition states that the waters – the 'fountains of the deep' – are relocated under the seventh earth and above the seventh heaven.

169. Ra'anan S. Bouston and Annette Yoshiko Reed, *Heavenly Realms and Earthly Realities in Late Antique Religions,* Cambridge University Press, 2004, p. 259.

170. Rig Veda Samhita 6.8.3: "two sustaining worlds – heaven and earth" and 6.8.7: "Adored Agni, present in the three worlds ... ." *Rig Veda Samhita*, translation according to Wilson, H.H. & Bhashya of Sayanacharya, edited by Arya, R.P. & Joshi, K.L., Parimal Publications: Delhi, 2005.

171. 2 Enoch, Greek T. Levi 2:1-5:3. Ra'anan S. Bouston and Annette Yoshiko Reed, *Heavenly Realms and Earthly Realities in Late Antique Religions,* Cambridge University Press, 2004, p. 259.

172. The three divisions are said to be earth, atmosphere and heaven; the twice seven are the fourteen worlds or planes (Yadupati).

173. John L. McKenzie, A Theology of the Old Testament, Doubleday, 1974, p. 199; also Robert A. Oden, "Cosmogony, Cosmology," in vol. 1 of ABD, ed. D. N. Freedman, Doubleday, 1992, pp. 1162-71

174. Bar-Ilan 2003, Bar-Ilan, Meir, *The Numerology of Genesis* (in Hebrew), Rehovot: Association for Jewish Astrology and Numerology, 2003, p. 105; Shulamit Valler, Haifa University, *Book Review of The Numerology of Genesis* (in Hebrew), Bar-Ilan, Meir, Rehovot: Association for Jewish Astrology and Numerology, 2003, p. vi, 218. Hardcover. ISBN 9659062001, p. 2, http://www.bookreviews.org/pdf/4331_4314.pdf

175. The Academy of Jerusalem – Torah from Zion Project, *The New Israeli Genesis Exegesis, (The Book of Genesis as a Redemptive Scenario and Rebiographic Guide),* Bible Overview - Gn (Genesis) - Gn 1. http://www.interlevensbeschouwelijk.be/otgn10.htm. Retrieved 27 November 2011.

176. Gordon J. Wenham, Thomas Nelson, *Word Biblical Commentary,* Vol. 1: Genesis 1-15, 1987, p. 6

177. *Ibid.*, p. 7

178. Geoffrey W. Bromiley, *Seven Last Words,* The International Standard Bible Encyclopedia, Wm. B. Eerdmans Publishing Company, 1995, p. 426

179. Norriss S. Hetherington, *Cosmology: Historical, Literary, Philosophical, Religious, and Scientific Perspectives,* Garland Publishing, Inc., 1993, p. 44; Adela Yarbro Collins, *Cosmology and Eschatology in Jewish and Christian Apocalypticism*, Brill, 2000, p. 28.

180. Thomas McEvilly, *The Shape of Ancient Thought: comparative studies in Greek and Indian philosophies,* Allworth Press, 2002, pp. 137-138;

Kaushitaki Upanishad 1.2; Karen Armstrong, *A History of God,* 1993, p. 214; Gershom Scholem, *Major Trends in Jewish Mysticism,* Schocken, 1995, pp. 50-51

181.	The oldest of extant references to three heavens is that by Paul in 2 Corinthians. However, the Testament of Levi III contains a description of the seven heavens (but not earths). It's a very old and enigmatic document. It seems to be a Christian version of an earlier Jewish text. As a Christian document it was written about 200 AD. But, the Jewish version could be as old as 100 BC. George J. Brooke, *The Dead Sea Scrolls and the New Testament,* Augsburg Fortress Publishers, 2005, p.142; William D. Barrick, *Scrolls from the Judean Desert,* The Master's Seminary, http://www.drbarrick.org/Website%20Files/Scrolls.pdf. Retrieved August 17, 2011.

182.	Jonathan T. Pennington and Sean M. McDonough, *Cosmology and New Testament Theology,* T&T Clark, 2008, p. 92.

183.	Interestingly, other authors of the New Testament don't articulate their cosmology precisely anywhere, either. (Jonathan T. Pennington and Sean M. McDonough, *Cosmology and New Testament Theology,* T&T Clark, 2008, pp. 189-190) This is also evidence that it was not new. It was none other than what was traditionally known, the scheme of seven heavens and seven earths.

184.	Barbara A. Holdrege, Veda and Torah: transcending the textuality of scripture, Sri Satguru Publications, 1996, pp. 12-13.

185.	*The Book of Legends, Sefer Ha-Aggadah, Legends from the Talmud and Midrash,* Edited by Hayim Nahman Bialik and Yehoshua Hana Ravnitzky, translated by William G. Braude, Schoken Books, New York, 1992, p. xxi & 3

186.	*The Book of Legends, Sefer Ha-Aggadah, Legends from the Talmud and Midrash,* Edited by Hayim Nahman Bialik and Yehoshua Hana Ravnitzky, translated by William G. Braude, Schoken Books, New York, 1992, p. xix; Angelo S. Rappoport, *Myth and Legend of Ancient Israel,* vol. 1, KTAV Publishing House, Inc, 1966, p. xiii

187.	Peter Watson, *Ideas,* New York, NY: HarperCollins Publishers, p. 170

188.	The vast majority of the text discusses religious law concerning rituals and conduct.

189.	Some of the descriptions of the world given by the ancient Israelites is compiled from Louis Ginzberg, *The Legends of the Jews,* 1909, Vol. I, pp. 11-17; Angelo S. Rappoport, *Myth and Legend of Ancient Israel,* vol. vi, KTAV Publishing House, Inc, 1966, pp. 9-10; Abodah Zarah, 3b.

190.	Angelo S. Rappoport, *Myth and Legend of Ancient Israel,* vol. vi, KTAV Publishing House, Inc, 1966, pp. 9-10; Abodah Zarah, 3b.

191.	*Come and Hear,* Babylonian Talmud: Tractate 'Abodah Zarah, Folio 3a, http://www.come-and-hear.com/zarah/zarah_3.html#3b_23. Retrieved Oct 3 2011

192. An accomplished Yogi can also see, listen, and lift objects from hundreds of thousands of leagues away. *Vachanamruta, Vartal 13; Yoga Sutra 3.35, 48* say a fully accomplished Yogi attains omniscience and omnipotence.

193. Norriss S. Hetherington, *Cosmology: Historical, Literary, Philosophical, Religious, and Scientific Perspectives,* Garland Publishing, Inc., 1993, p. 27; John H. Walton, Ancient Near Eastern Thought and the Old Testament, Baker Academic, 2006, p. 166; Thomas McEvilly, *The Shape of Ancient Thought: comparative studies in Greek and Indian philosophies,* Allworth Press, 2002, p. 35

194. The cosmic egg is clarified by slightly later Yogis as having seven or eight investing envelopes.

195. Brihadaranyaka Upanishad, 4.2.2; Shatapatha Brahmana, 6:1.1.2.11; Aitareya Upanishad, 1:3.14; Aitareya Brahmana, 3:33 end, 7:30 end.

196. A complementary explanation involves the age old phenomenon of UFOs. What are these Unidentified Flying Objects? Who are their occupants? If they are advanced life forms from other planets in the universe, could they have communicated their superior knowledge to human beings thousands of years ago? Such incidences could account for the enormous knowledge of the universe the ancients possessed. Indeed, the ancient Yogis often narrated conversations that occurred between divinities or 'heavenly beings' and humans. It's noteworthy that both the Yoga and Biblical literature abound with such accounts of angels and archangels (devas and mahadevas correspondingly in the Yoga Literature) visiting Earth as messengers and "ministering or serving spirits" (Hebrews 1:14) In the Yoga Literature, these beings commonly arrive from the sky, often in brilliant or fiery vehicles, sometimes visible to the human eye. They have from time to time mentored and ministered to humanity's needs and bequeathed some of the wonderful truths of the cosmos you have seen in this book, and together with that, the meaning of human life. In the Yoga Literature, Brahma is described to have visited Earth on a number of occasions and so have archangels in the Bible. Strikingly, in 1826, in the earliest documented mass sighting of a UFO in India, the preeminent Yogi Shri Swaminarayan, expounded along similar lines upon the following incident: A large congregation of monks and laymen had gathered before him in the evening. After his discourse, a brilliant ball of light appeared in the sky above them. The luminous sphere separated into three, remained there for a moment, and then disappeared into the distance. Members of the congregation were astounded and asked the Yogi what the spheres were. "Every evening," he replied, "Brahma, Vishnu, and Shiva come here to marvel at the congregation of monks and to listen to these talks. But today, by the Lord's wish you were able to see them along with their flying vehicles." Shri Swaminarayan, Vachanamruta, Jetalpur 5, Swaminarayan Aksharpith, English Translation, 2006, pp. 695-696.

INDEX

INDEX

CPSIA information can be obtained at www.ICGtesting.com
Printed in the USA
LVOW042140220612

287320LV00001B/20/P